FEMINIST THEOLOGY/CHRISTIAN THEOLOGY

FEMINIST THEOLOGY/CHRISTIAN THEOLOGY

In Search of Method

Pamela Dickey Young

FORTRESS PRESS   MINNEAPOLIS

FEMINIST THEOLOGY/CHRISTIAN THEOLOGY
In Search of Method

Scripture quotations unless otherwise noted are from the Revised Standard Version of the Bible, copyright © 1946, 1952, and 1971 by the Division of Christian Education of the National Council of Churches.

Cover design: Pollock Haro

Library of Congress Cataloging-in-Publication Data

Young, Pamela Dickey, 1955-
    Feminist theology/Christian theology : in search of method /
Pamela Dickey Young.
        p.   cm.
    Includes index.
    ISBN 0-8006-2402-5
    1. Feminist theology.   I. Title.
BT83.55.Y68   1990
230'.082—dc20

89-36062
CIP

The paper used in this publication meets the minimum requirements of American National Standard for Information Sciences—Permanence of Paper for Printed Library Materials, ANSI Z329.48-1984. ∞™

Manufactured in the U.S.A.   AF 1-2402

94   93   92   91   90   1   2   3   4   5   6   7   8   9   10

CONTENTS

Preface   7

1/The Feminist Challenge and Theological Method   11
    The Feminist Challenge to Theology   11
    General Feminist Agreement   15
    Theological Method   17
    Structure of the Book   21

2/Some Feminist Methodologies   23
    A New Magisterium   24
    Feminist Eclecticism   31
    Norms from Christian Tradition   40

3/Women's Experience as Source and Norm
    of Theology   49
    Women's Experience as a Source   56
    Women's Experience as Norm   62
    Women's Experience and Schüssler Fiorenza,
        Ruether, Russell   67

4/The Place of Christian Tradition
    in a Christian Feminist Theology   71
    Christian Tradition as Source   71
    Christian Tradition as Norm   73
    How Should Christian Tradition Be Normative?   80
    Why Such a Norm Can Be Useful for Feminists   90

Contents

5/The Method Enacted: Christ and Church   95
        Christology   95
        Ecclesiology   106
        Conclusion   113

Epilogue   115

Notes   119

Index   129

PREFACE

Can one be both Christian and feminist at the same time? This question is still one of the central issues for feminist theology. As feminists have pointed out over and over again, the Christian church has condoned and even fostered the oppression of women. Because of this, some feminists have decided to abandon Christianity in favor of other religious options that are less ambiguous in their treatment of women. Others have sought to remain within the tradition and work for change, using feminist critical tools as their main point of departure, yet finding something within Christian tradition that is liberating and worth preserving. In all these discussions, a variety of understandings of both "feminism" and "Christian tradition" have emerged.

What does a feminist Christian theology or Christian feminist theology look like? How does one set out to construct such a theology? My main aim in this book is, in dialogue with other understandings, to set out a way to bring women's experience and Christian tradition together in a theological method that might be useful for the feminist struggling with the symbols of Christianity and the Christian struggling with the claims of feminism. The method proposed here is simply one way among many to do feminist Christian theology, but it is a way that I hope will be helpful to some.

As I hope to show, I am optimistic about the possibility of a Christian feminism and therefore of a Christian feminist theology. This optimism is not, however, born of a naïveté that has not seen other options or refuses to grapple with the hardest questions. I continue to struggle with the Christian tradition, wanting to give it the best possible formulation in light of the questions feminism must raise. I remain within the Christian tradition, yet I understand why others feel they must leave.

Many feminists are "self-taught" in the sense that they have not themselves had feminist teachers; their feminism has first been learned from personal experience and the writings of others. Such has been my lot. And so, first and foremost, my debts are to those feminists who wrote of their experiences in their theology. It was through Rosemary Radford Ruether's book *New Woman/New Earth* that I began to realize the force and necessity of feminist theological thought. Her work and that of Letty Russell and Elisabeth Schüssler Fiorenza have been enormously important as touchstones for my own work. Even though my methodological position differs from each of theirs, I would never have come to any feminist position without them. Now, happily, there is so much feminist work available that one cannot acknowledge it all, and much of it has been a lifeline to me and to other feminists who still number very few in faculties of theology or in local church organizations.

Many of my colleagues and students at Queen's Theological College have been involved in discussion of parts of this book along the way and I am grateful for their interest and encouragement. The students in my class on feminist theology during the 1988-89 academic year read a version of the manuscript and offered good commentary and helpful suggestions. Two students in particular, Paul Clarkson and Barbara Horricks, as well as Linda Thomas, a member of the support staff in the Department of Religion at Queen's University, have my thanks for helping in a variety of ways to prepare the manuscript.

J. Michael West of Fortress Press has been an interested and supportive editor and I thank him for that.

I also wish to acknowledge and to thank my teacher and friend Schubert M. Ogden, whose theology has profoundly influenced my theological thought. My debt to him is evident in these pages.

To my mother, Gwendolyn Dickey, who has supported me in every choice I have ever made, and to my husband, John Young, who has been theological co-traveler from the very beginning of my theological education, I am deeply grateful.

Pamela Dickey Young

1/
THE FEMINIST CHALLENGE
AND THEOLOGICAL METHOD

In her plenary address to the American Academy of Religion in 1984, Rosemary Radford Ruether stated that it was time for feminist theology to enter a new stage; to move beyond its first two stages of criticizing existing traditions and attempting to state these traditions in new ways to dealing seriously and explicitly with questions of theological method and norms.[1] Her point was that patriarchal theology would never be fully challenged unless it was challenged not merely in its details but at its very roots.

Theologians are constantly faced with many basic questions about the nature of their calling. Along with getting on with the actual task of doing theology, they must always be ready to reflect on what is, in fact, the task of the theologian. How and why do they do what they do? Feminist theologians are doubly called to this sort of reflection if they want to change the very nature of theology as it has been up to the present.

This volume is one attempt to enter the new stage for which Ruether calls.

The Feminist Challenge to Theology

Feminist theology draws on the broader project of feminist theory. Although feminist theorists differ in the ways they analyze women's oppression, they do agree on certain fundamental themes. Arising out of feminist consciousness and feminist political and

11

social action, feminist theory recognizes the systemic oppression of women and encourages women to name their oppression and to ponder its sources. Various feminist theories see those sources differently, yet all stress the necessity of considering these sources and positing possible solutions to oppression according to their differing analyses. Feminist theorists see the importance of providing a theoretical accounting of women's situation so as to understand the commonality of women's oppression on the one hand while not denying the variety of women's experiences on the other.

Some of the main areas that feminist theory points up for analysis are sexuality, socialization, production (all work paid and unpaid), and reproduction (including child rearing).[2] How "woman" is constructed by patriarchy in each of these areas is the catalyst for theoretical reflection in economic, social, political, and cultural terms. Feminist theology takes part in feminist theory insofar as it takes on the task of analyzing the construction of "woman" and in particular adds its own theoretical reflections in ecclesiastical or religious terms.

The feminist challenge to theology is well documented in what is coming to be an enormous body of literature. Many writers have correctly pointed to two stages in most of the feminist theological work to date. There was the first stage of critique, and the second stage of reconstruction.

In the first stage feminists began the necessary documentation of the roles and images of women in the history of Christian tradition.[3] They pointed out how very few women were seen as important to the Christian tradition and how the few women who were portrayed in the tradition were often seen as negative images or examples (like Eve). They also pointed to the fact that women, not as specific characters, but as a group, were portrayed as dangerous or evil.

The biblical documents were shown to be clearly products of patriarchal times, with feminists citing, for example, certain passages where women were regarded as property or told to

12

keep silent. History records many inglorious instances of Christianity's failure to treat women as full and whole human beings. Tertullian spoke of women as the "devil's gateway," and Thomas Aquinas, following Aristotle, spoke of women as "misbegotten men."[4] Women have often been cast in the male-defined roles of wife/mother, virgin, and whore. They have been seen as the (so-called) temptress, Eve, or they have been asked to emulate the virgin mother (physically impossible).

In this first stage as well, feminists began to point out how women's absence, the failure to take women into account, had affected theological thinking. Important issues began to surface, such as analyzing the effect of a tradition that had almost exclusively used male images for God and asking what difference it made to the church that only half its members were considered fully human (especially when it came to eligibility for ordination). Every theological doctrine and concept had to be examined anew in light of the growing awareness that women had been oppressed in the church at least as systematically as in other parts of society.

The second stage—reconstruction—followed closely on the first.[5] Indeed, critique continues and must continue parallel to reconstruction so that one is continually reminded of the need for reconstruction. And, just as no area of theology is exempt from critique, so none is considered to be dealt with so definitively that it is exempt from reconstruction.

The reconstruction of theology with feminist questions in mind has given rise to new avenues of thought. Feminist theologians are not content only to point to the negative or absent history of women. Feminist historians are seeking to recover lost histories of women; they are seeing that women are often present in places where their presence has gone unnoticed for centuries; they are presuming women's presence. If one considers the writings of women of the past important and worthy of study, there is material from the hands of women to be found. One recovers as much of women's religious history as one can to see what forgotten roles women may have played and to see what the lives of these past women may have to say to us today. One asks new questions of history, one begins to think of religious history in new ways, not just as the history of councils and important leaders, but as the everyday history of the faithful, women and men.

The process of reconstruction also involves the reconstruction of various doctrines as these have been traditionally explicated in systematic theology. Feminist theologians seek to revise various doctrines in ways that take account of women's presence, of women's experience. They also revise these doctrines so that they will not contribute to the continued oppression of women.

The doctrine of God, for example, is no longer a doctrine of the all-male God. Rather, God is seen in a variety of images, either in gender-neutral terms or in both female and male terms.[6] A new understanding of church is formulated, which includes an understanding of ministry that is broader than just ordination, and which questions the hierarchical power of most institutional church structures.[7]

New images of women are formulated, either out of the material of history or of story, images of powerful women, images of strong women, who can be called on to inspire us to action in the present. Sarah and Hagar are remembered. Mary the mother of Jesus is no longer the "gentle Mary, meek and mild" of our Sunday school days, but the independent woman who chooses to cooperate with God. Eve is not the source of all evil but the woman who weighs and chooses knowledge over ignorance. Images of such women can serve as role models for contemporary women; the past, whether historical or legendary, can encourage faith and action in the present.

New liturgies are constructed where women's stories are told and celebrated, where women are more than passive recipients of the actions of males; they are active in shaping what happens. In such new liturgies, the worship experience grows out of the collective experience of the whole community. Worship is not used as a tool for one group to assert power over another. It becomes instead a collective experience of love of God and of one another, where no one is excluded or found less worthy than another.

General Feminist Agreement

Although feminist theologies vary in their structure, form, emphases, and so forth, there are some basic agreements among feminist theologians. First, traditional theology is patriarchal. It has been written, almost totally, *by* men. It has been formulated, despite claims to universality, as though maleness were the normative form of humanity, and thus, it has been *about* men. When theology is specifically "about" women, it is about them in negative ways, not as part of the category "human," but as negative exceptions to that category, as deviant. Theology has also been written *for* men, that is, with men assumed as the primary audience of readers and thinkers. And, even if the above points might be countered in isolated cases, theology has been created, in Western culture, in a patriarchal social structure that shapes its ideas and gives an aura of "rightness" and a social sanction to the ecclesiastical status quo.

Second, the obverse of the first point, traditional theology has ignored or caricatured women and women's experience. Women were not considered to have anything important to say. Some books by women, when read as anonymous works, were considered important until it was discovered who their authors were. Women's authorship immediately discounted the value of a work. Women were not seen as subjects of theological anthropology. The generic "man" in Christian theology was really the male. Women who appeared in Scripture or tradition were often simply ignored or their roles downplayed to fit patriarchal expectations of women.

Mary Magdalene, first among the apostles in the stories of the resurrection, is rarely seen that way in Christian tradition, largely because it was presumed that a woman could not play such an important role.[8] Junia in Romans 16, became Junianus for the same reason.[9] Often, if women were not ignored, they were caricatured, made to fit male views of women as unstable, flighty, ignorant, and so on. Again, Mary Magdalene is a good example, for, completely without scriptural warrant, she is named a prostitute in the traditions about her.

Whether "universal" theological concepts such as those of sin and salvation really applied to women in the same way they applied to men was not considered. Yet women were assumed to be those most prone to sin and temptation, and here Eve was usually cited as the prime example.

If women had nothing important to say, neither were they considered to be the main readers or consumers of theology. Too much learning, theological learning included, was considered detrimental to women's reproductive work.

The third area of agreement among feminist theologians is that the patriarchal nature of theology has had deleterious consequences for women. For, in addition to being shaped by its culture through the ages, Christian theology has often been a major force in shaping culture. So there was a circular problem. Ignoring women and perpetuating unfavorable images when women were mentioned at all both arose from and contributed to patriarchal culture in church and in society in general. These lost or caricatured images of women and the refusal to consider women as proper subjects or writers of theology affected the attitudes of both church and society toward women and their capabilities; they affected the roles it was considered possible for women to play in both church and society; they constricted women's development as fully adult human beings.

Finally, feminist theologians all agree on one element in the solution to the above-mentioned problems. Women must begin to be theologians, they must refuse to write only about or for men. They must question the patriarchal mind-set that grants legitimacy to traditional theologizing. They must do theology in such a way that the history of women and women's experiences make a difference and can be seen to make a difference. Women must become equal shapers of the theological enterprise.

Theological Method

There is no unanimity in feminist theology when it comes to the articulation and use of a particular theological methodology. This lack of unanimity is not a weakness; indeed, it can be seen as a strength, testifying to the richness and depth of feminist theological thought and opinion, especially given the areas of agreement noted above.

Nonetheless, the question of method is all-important in theology, for, whether explicitly articulated or implicitly assumed, one's theological method in large part determines one's theological outcome. When a person is explicit about the theological method being used it makes for consistency and coherence in theology. Sometimes, of course, we come to understand the methods we are using only after we have engaged in theologizing and then reflect on what it is we have done. Once we understand the methods, we are compelled to use whatever criteria we have settled upon consistently, not to change as we go along. For example, theologians must be consistent in their use of Scripture. It will do no good to complain about those who cite Scripture out of context, only to "proof-text" with other texts that fit one's own case.

Mary Daly writes about the "tyranny of methodolatry,"[10] by which she means that methods often encourage us to ask only the questions that have been asked before, rendering all other questions and answers "nondata."[11] But a method need not be a mold that squeezes everything into its own terms. Method is not separate from the data that give rise to a need for method.

Methods only arise as there is a need to account for something. And one always has to reckon with the possibility that the available data may not fit the method.

Yet method does give a framework to thought, and if a search for method arises from explicitly feminist commitments, "nondata" become data. The search for method that is undertaken here is a search that sees itself in continuity with feminist theory, the desire to account for something within a particular framework, the framework of the understanding and unmasking of patriarchy.

Methods have their limitations. They cannot always account for all that must be said. Yet if theologians are explicit about the methodologies they employ, they give their readers insights into what they as theologians think is most important. An explicitly articulated theological method lays bare what is at stake in any given theology. It shows readers how the theologian arrived at the product set before them. It gives insight into the process of theology. When they are setting out their methodological comments, theologians tell their readers just what sort of theology they understand themselves to be providing. What are its main emphases? Does it understand itself in terms of any of the usual labels or does it see itself as proposing something completely new or different? Is this a feminist theology, and, if so, what does "feminist" mean here? Is it a Christian or Jewish theology or a theology of some other sort? These are just a few of the questions that might be answered. Such an insight into the process allows the reader to enter more quickly into what follows, with eyes more widely open.

If theologians are clear in their own minds about the methodologies they employ, they can make the strongest possible cases for various aspects of their theologies. In the event of theological disagreement or dispute, then, it may at least be possible to demonstrate how one's own theology grows out of certain methodological suppositions, shifting the argument to a different plane and showing how one's position is consistent with one's entire theological point of view.

Theological method here means some answer to the question, What is theology and how does one get on with the process of theologizing? In articulating a theological method, theologians tell their readers what they understand themselves to be doing; they explain how they understand the theological task, including perhaps most especially what they mean by theology. Is theology to be seen primarily as a reflective process or as activity or as some combination of the two? What is the particular object of theological action or reflection, both in terms of its goal and in terms of material from a tradition or traditions on which it is based? Who are theology's subjects? To whom is the theology directed?

One way to enter the discussion of theological method is to be concerned with the sources from which a given theology arises or is drawn and with the norms that the theologian uses to argue for the adequacy of her or his own theology or to judge the adequacy of other theologies. Both sources and norms can vary widely.

Source here means, basically, any element that enters into the formulation of one's theology, anything that informs one's theology. Such elements might be textual material or other sorts of data from within a given religious tradition; material peripheral to or outside a particular religious tradition, but that is still deemed relevant for one reason or another; the experience of particular groups of people; and human experience in general or specific types of human experiences.

Norm here means a specific criterion or set of criteria by which any given theological sources or formulations are judged to be adequate or inadequate for theology in general or for the type of theology being done, and which is used as the structuring principle for a theologian's own theology. Some of the many criteria that have been used as norms in Christian theology are

Scripture, the magisterium of pope and bishops, the historical Jesus, women's experience, and human reason.

When the question of methodology for feminist theology is raised, one of the key issues is the relationship between past tradition and present experience. To deal with methodology in terms of sources and norms illuminates this relationship. From what sources, past and present, should feminist theologizing be done? Even more important is the question of norms. By what criterion or set of criteria should a feminist theology be judged to be adequate? What norms will be employed in feminist theologizing? In what ways are these norms related to tradition? If the feminist theology claims to be a Christian theology, in what ways are these norms related to the Christian past? In what ways are these norms drawn from the present, especially for a feminist theology, from the present experience of women, so long neglected by traditional theology?

It is this interplay between past and present that most interests me here. Many of the current Christian feminist theologies, although they use the Christian past as *source* for their theologies, do not employ that same past as *norm*. Instead, they see women's experience as the only norm for a feminist theology. This book maintains that any theology claiming to be both feminist and Christian should draw its norms both from the Christian tradition of which it sees itself a part and from the long-overlooked experience of women.

It is the question of the interrelationship between past tradition and present experience in Christian feminist theology, the question of continuity and change, that will take center stage here. In what ways should a Christian feminist theology be continuous with past Christian tradition? With which Christian tradition or traditions should it be continuous? In what ways should a Christian feminist theology reformulate, rework, and rethink these traditions in order to deal with the pressing questions of the present? What should be the norm or norms that determine how all these questions are answered?

My own interest in the question of methodology in feminist theology arises for several reasons. As a feminist, I am in agreement with the feminist consensus outlined above and thus I see the need for theology to take women's history and experience with utmost seriousness, to grapple with the issues raised by feminist critique. Thus the method I outline must be feminist. It cannot allow theology to get away with fostering the oppression of women in the guise of being true to some static view of Christian reality.

But as a Christian, and a Protestant Christian, I also see the need to be explicit about the normative value of parts of the Christian tradition. I do not embrace the traditional *sola scriptura* of Protestantism, but, although many feminist theologians today would disagree, I do see a need to draw norms from the Christian tradition for a Christian feminist theology. I am not oblivious to the problems that such a position creates for the feminist. Yet I hope to make clear that my own understanding of what it means to do Christian feminist theology leads me to put a more central and normative emphasis on Christian tradition than has sometimes been done in feminist theology.

An additional contribution I seek to make in this book is toward the further definition of "women's experience." The term is bandied about by countless writers (feminist and nonfeminist alike), but it has not often been explicated at length.

Structure of the Book

The general goal of this book, then, is to make a contribution to ongoing feminist discussions of theological methodology, specifically methodology for a Christian feminist theology. Chapter 2 of the book will outline three important ways of relating Christian tradition and women's experience. Categorized by what each takes to be normative, they are: the appeal to the magisterium of women's experience, the use of a feminist eclecticism that picks what it needs from a variety of places, and the drawing of norms from both women's experience and the Christian tradition. I choose three theologians, Elisabeth Schüssler Fiorenza, Rosemary Radford Ruether, and Letty Russell as examples of these positions, but others could be offered.[12] The three have been chosen because each has written extensively on the question at hand and because their work is widely known and readily accessible. The outlines of their methods focus on whether and how present experience and past traditions are sources and norms of theology and give three differing ways to think about methodology.

Chapters 3 and 4 will then take up in more detail the questions of present experience and past tradition respectively. In both chapters my own formulations of these two methodological concerns will take place in dialogue with those outlined in the second chapter. The third chapter will focus in large part specifically on the topic of women's experience, which is the primary category feminists have added to theological methodology in an effort to broaden theology's inclusivity. Theological thought that does not take women's experience into consideration is simply incredible to most women. Therefore, this discussion of women's experience will be set in the context of a discussion of what credibility means for Christian theology. Just what the category of women's experience entails will be explored, including how it relates to other experience, as will questions of how it might function as source and norm in Christian theology.

The question of how feminist theology is in continuity with the Christian tradition is the subject of the fourth chapter. It seeks to give one answer to the question, How can theology be both feminist and Christian at the same time?

The fifth chapter will apply, in broad outline form, the methodology suggested in chapters 3 and 4 to the theological themes of Christ and church. In the epilogue I talk of the relationship between theology and personal quest in my own life.

2/
SOME FEMINIST METHODOLOGIES

There are numerous ways in which Christian tradition and women's experience might combine as source material for theology. Yet if one concentrates on the question of what is normative as a way to understand what is happening in feminist theology from a methodological point of view, three main emphases can be seen.

Some feminist theologians today, regardless of the sources they use, appeal to an alternative magisterium, one drawn in some way from women's experience, as their central or final norm. Some feminist theologians practice a feminist eclecticism that draws on a variety of sources and norms. Still other feminist theologians appeal, in concert with sources and norms drawn from women's experience, to sources and norms explicitly taken from the Christian tradition.

But if one talks about theological methodology without recourse to specific examples, one runs the risk of being thought so abstract as to be speaking of nothing in particular. To help avoid this danger and to provide some concrete starting points for my own methodological remarks, I will outline three models for understanding the interaction between Christian tradition and women's experience in feminist theology. The models I have chosen (as exemplified by three theologians) represent differing points of emphasis rather than hard and fast divisions; feminist theologians do not always fit neatly into one category or another.

The three theologians I have chosen are Elisabeth Schüssler Fiorenza, Rosemary Radford Ruether, and Letty Russell. I have chosen them for several reasons. First, of course, all three are prominent feminist authors who have contributed much to the development of feminist theology. Second, they all consider themselves within Christianity rather than outside it, and my concern here is specifically with Christian feminist theology. Third, they have all written on a number of different theological themes, allowing one to see their methodologies at work in a variety of contexts and concerning a variety of questions. Schüssler Fiorenza appeals to the alternative magisterium of women-church as the norm for Christian theology. Ruether at one time appealed to the prophetic-liberating tradition as one of the main norms of theology, but now her position tends to an eclecticism or feminist ecumenism that picks and chooses what it needs. Russell appeals to the example of Jesus and the notion of a utopian future as normative alongside norms drawn from women's experience.

A New Magisterium

Elisabeth Schüssler Fiorenza points to a new magisterium, that of women-church. She is a Roman Catholic feminist biblical scholar, and thus primarily interested in feminist biblical interpretation rather than in writing a theology. Nonetheless her methodological remarks are important for feminist theology, not least because so many feminist theologians have followed her methodological lead, especially in what should be normative in a Christian feminist theology. Through her many writings, in particular *In Memory of Her*, she has awakened others to the need for feminist readings of the Bible and feminist theology.

Schüssler Fiorenza recognizes that there are many possible feminist theologies, and she sees her own theology in continuity with other liberation theologies that criticize the status quo. As a theology of liberation, it begins with the experience of women who are struggling for liberation from patriarchy and calls for the eradication of this oppression. The preferential option for the poor becomes a preferential option for all women, especially poor women. A feminist theology of liberation has as one of its main goals wholeness, the overcoming of dualisms such as mind and body, male and female, technology and nature, and it insists that wholeness is attainable only when hierarchy is overcome. As a critical theology, feminist theology censures patriarchal religion and seeks alternative theological formulations.

Not only does Schüssler Fiorenza's feminist theology begin with women's experience of oppression, but this experience functions as the central focus and evaluative norm of her theology and other theologies of this type.[1] Because the Bible has been used to perpetuate the oppression of women, because it has been written by men out of a patriarchal mindset and therefore is not unambiguously liberating, Schüssler Fiorenza thinks that one cannot look to the biblical witness itself for the central norm of Christian faith.[2] The only adequate norm is one that supports and ensures the overcoming of women's oppression and fosters women's religious quest for self-affirmation and self-determination. "I would therefore suggest that the revelatory canon for theological evaluation of biblical androcentric traditions and their subsequent interpretations cannot be derived from the Bible itself but can only be formulated in and through women's struggle for liberation from all patriarchal oppression."[3]

In *Bread Not Stone* Schüssler Fiorenza speaks of a feminist critical hermeneutics as deriving its canon of inspired truth and revelation "*not* from the biblical writings but from the contemporary struggle of women against racism, sexism and poverty as oppressive systems of patriarchy and from its systematic explorations in feminist theory."[4]

Also in *Bread Not Stone*, Schüssler Fiorenza shows that "revelatory" and "Christian" are parallel terms. "What it means to be a Christian woman is not defined by essential female nature or timeless biblical revelation, but grows out of the concrete social structures and cultural-religious mechanisms of women's oppression as well as our struggles for liberation, selfhood, and transcendence."[5] Thus, for Schüssler Fiorenza, the criterion used to evaluate biblical texts is whether or not the text serves to liberate women. A text is accepted as revealed, and therefore normatively Christian, if it serves the cause of women's liberation from oppression. The biblical texts in and of themselves cannot be seen to be normative, nor can any canon or norm be derived from the biblical texts.

She uses biblical texts in the service of liberation, and she accepts as useful only those portions of the Bible that fit her criterion.

> A feminist theological interpretation of the Bible that has as its canon the liberation of women from oppressive sexist structures, institutions, and internalized values must, therefore, maintain that only the nonsexist and nonandrocentric traditions of the Bible and the nonoppressive traditions of biblical interpretation have the theological authority of revelation if the Bible is not to continue as a tool for the oppression of women.[6]

All biblical texts "must be tested as to their feminist liberating content and function in their historical and contemporary contexts."[7]

It is the *ekklesia* of women, or women-church, the "movement of self-identified women and women-identified men in biblical religion"[8] that functions as the magisterium for feminist theology, adjudicating theological claims as adequate or not according to whether or not they oppress or liberate women. "The locus or place of divine revelation and grace is therefore not the Bible or the tradition of a patriarchal church but the *ekklesia* of women and the lives of women who live the 'option for our women selves.' "[9] The goal of the *ekklesia* of women is "women's religious self-affirmation, power, and liberation from all patriarchal alienation, marginalization, and oppression."[10]

Schüssler Fiorenza distinguishes between Scripture as archetype and as prototype. For her, an archetypal use of Scripture is to see it as a finished, unchanging, and unchangeable document of the past. When one uses Scripture as archetype, one identifies the text with revelation, one cannot take today's questions and concerns into account. To use Scripture as prototype is to see it as opening from the past into the present; it is not to confine revelation to the past, but to see a continuity between past revelation and present revelation.[11] To try to find the norm for revelation within the biblical texts themselves is to use the Bible as archetype.

Schüssler Fiorenza criticizes Letty Russell and Rosemary Ruether for being "neo-orthodox," and for ignoring the oppressive and androcentric elements in Scripture in their desire to derive a norm from Scripture itself. Only those portions of Scripture that transcend patriarchy can be used by and for Christian women, and even these texts themselves are not normative, but are made normative by women-church.

> [F]eminist theologies introduce a radical shift into all forms of traditional theology insofar as they insist that the central commitment and accountability for feminist theologians is not to *the* church as a male institution but to women in the churches, not to *the* tradition as such but to a feminist transformation of Christian traditions, not to *the* Bible on the whole but to the liberating word of God coming to articulation in the biblical writings.[12]

Despite the fact that she does not think that one can derive a norm for theology from the Bible, Schüssler Fiorenza does not want to dispense with the biblical witness entirely and opt for some other tradition or for some new form of religiosity. First and foremost among her reasons for not abandoning the Bible is her unwillingness to allow it to be used only by those who would reinforce patriarchy. To give up one's biblical heritage is to permit what has been taken to be its hierarchical view to stand unchallenged.[13] One must look seriously at the biblical texts to see if there really might not be women's histories that have been overlooked. And indeed, in *In Memory of Her*, Schüssler Fiorenza amply demonstrates that precisely this is the case, that if we look to the biblical texts with questions about women's histories in mind, we are surprised by what we find there.

Also, because of the continuing influence of the Bible in the Western world and because many women continue to find resources for positive self-identity within these texts, feminists cannot simply ignore them and still claim to want to be in solidarity with all women.[14] Solidarity requires that one try to understand women where they are in their search for liberation, or where they might begin that search.

Schüssler Fiorenza realizes that feminists are not simply ahistorical beings who spring out of nowhere. Many feminists have religious roots, and for many feminists these roots lie deep in Christianity. Women who have found Christianity meaningful in the past are not always willing simply to let it go when they become feminists. "Thus to reclaim early Christian history as women's own past and to insist that women's history is an integral part of early Christian historiography imply the search for roots, for solidarity with our foresisters, and finally for the memory of their sufferings, struggles, and powers as women."[15] The desire, then, is not to relinquish one's past, but to transform it insofar as one discovers things about it that one did not know before and insofar as one reinterprets other elements of it. Feminists can explore how the Bible can be and has been used against them to foster oppression as well as it can be and has been used to reject oppression.

Although, according to Schüssler Fiorenza, feminists do not find the evaluative norm for Christian theology in the biblical texts, neither can they give up these texts and still remain Christian. "Since feminist theology as a Christian theology is bound to its charter documents in Scripture, it must formulate this problem [of Christian feminism] with reference to the Bible and biblical revelation."[16]

What feminists need to do is to teach and foster a new use of Scripture, so it can and will be used only in the service of liberation for women and for others who are oppressed, and so it will never be used in the further service of oppression. "Christian (and in my case Roman Catholic) feminists also do not relinquish their biblical roots and heritage. As the *ekklesia* of women, we claim the center of Christian faith and community in a feminist process of transformation."[17]

Schüssler Fiorenza sees her own option for a liberating canon as an option that is very much in line with the Christian tradition. A feminist critical theology of liberation "follows Augustine, Thomas, and the Vatican Council II in formulating a criterion or canon that limits inspired truth and revelation to matters pertaining to the salvation, freedom and liberation of all, especially of women."[18]

What counts as word of God, then, is only that which liberates women, and so not all of Scripture is word of God. The Bible does have liberating power, but only in some of its passages, or the traditions that lie behind them, and therefore it is not a norm for theology, but only a resource on which the Christian community can draw. One of the ways in which the community can draw on that resource is to see how the texts have functioned in various Christian communities in the past. For instance, if texts recall people's experiences of God in the struggle against patriarchal oppression, then these texts might become paradigmatic for women-church.[19]

Schüssler Fiorenza advocates four basic hermeneutical approaches to Scripture.[20] First, a hermeneutics of suspicion assumes the androcentrism of biblical texts and their interpretations. A hermeneutics of proclamation judges the way in which the Bible can be used in the contemporary community of faith. It weeds out of liturgical use those texts that are oppressive for women. A hermeneutics of remembrance seeks to recover biblical traditions from a feminist perspective by asking new questions to see where in fact the women in biblical tradition are and what they are doing. By the hermeneutics of creative actualization women are enabled to enter biblical history through the historical imagination, artistic re-creation and ritual. The remnants, strands, and traditions that survive or can be inferred are forged into larger imaginative wholes through which women can experience the pain and the joy of their foresisters.

Given that Schüssler Fiorenza does not derive her theological norms in any way from Scripture, Jesus (whether the historical Jesus or the Jesus of the gospel kerygma) is not normative in her understanding of Christian theology. Nonetheless Jesus is important for women because the movement that began with and around him was an egalitarian movement in which God's future, the *basileia* was communicated and promised to all the people of Israel.[21] The God of Jesus was an inclusive God who welcomed and received all people.

The community of Jesus was a community of equals whom he called to faith in God. From these texts about Jesus, women can derive a positive sense of self-identity and a vision of an egalitarian society that might be. Women of today can experience a sense of solidarity with the women who gathered around Jesus.

The women of today who do experience that sense of solidarity, along with women-identified men, are women-church, the locus of divine revelation and grace. For Schüssler Fiorenza, true church is women-church, those who band together to struggle against oppression. Women-church strives for women's power and religious self-affirmation, their liberation, as well as the liberation of all from alienation, marginalization, and oppression.[22]

It is from women-church as ongoing Christian community, a community to which the biblical texts can speak today, that norms for theology are drawn. It is through women-church that the roots and structures of women's oppression are analyzed. The *ekklesia* of women is "the gathering of free and responsible citizens who have the power to articulate their own theology, to reclaim their own spirituality, and to determine their own and their sisters' religious life. As church we celebrate our religious powers and visions for change, we ritualize our struggles, and we share our strengths in nurturing one another."[23] Through women-church, God can be renamed, Christ can be reclaimed, and church can be reinterpreted, all in terms of women's experience of oppression.

For Schüssler Fiorenza, the final word on what counts as normative is as follows: "Instead of asking whether an approach is appropriate to the Scriptures and adequate to the human condition, one needs to test whether a theological model of biblical interpretation is *adequate* to the historical-literary methods of contemporary interpretation and *appropriate* to the struggle of the oppressed for liberation."[24] She wants to do a responsible job of interpreting the texts, and thus to employ historical-literary methods of interpretation in the most adequate way possible. In the end, however, whether or not the oppressed are liberated is the ultimate norm by which the Scriptures are judged.

Feminist Eclecticism

Some feminists come to the question of Christian tradition and women's experience by appealing to sources and norms for theology as these are needed to make particular points.[25] Rosemary Radford Ruether is one such feminist theologian. One can see her method as one in transition.

Ruether is also a Roman Catholic feminist theologian. Her work covers a broad range of topics from feminist religious history and constructive feminist theology to feminist revisionings of society. Here I deal only with her theological methodology and not with her many other contributions to feminist study of religion.

Ruether sees feminist theology as currently in its third stage. After first criticizing the masculine focus of traditional Christian theology and then seeking alternative feminist ways to restate this Christian theology, feminist theology is now at the point where it needs to reconsider and reexamine the norms and methods of theology.[26] Indeed, it was the need I myself experienced for a feminist articulation of theological method and norms that prompted this book.

For her, the crucial principle of any adequate feminist theology is that it promote the full humanity of women. "Whatever denies, diminishes, or distorts the full humanity of women is, therefore, appraised as not redemptive," it does not reflect the divine nor is it the message of an authentic redeemer.[27] The uniqueness of feminist theology lies not in its critical principle of full humanity, but in the fact that women claim this principle for themselves.[28] Feminist theology is also unique in the fact that it draws on and reflects women's experience—of themselves, of the divine, of the community and the world of which they are a part.

Ruether recognizes and explicitly states that the context or viewpoint from which she does her own theologizing is a Western, Christian context. She does not think that any one theology, feminist or otherwise, can claim to speak to and for all contexts. Like other feminist theologians, she is aware that her questions and her point of view arise out of her own background and experience. There is no one "objective" point of view outside all commitments or contextual influences.

At least since *Sexism and God-Talk* Ruether has articulated her sources for feminist theology as including some from outside the mainstream Christian tradition. By sources here she means material ("usable tradition") from which she has drawn themes and clues for her own theological formulations. Thus, the sources for her feminist theology include Scripture (both Hebrew and Christian), marginal and heretical Christian traditions, the dominant tradition in Christian theology, non-Christian Near Eastern and Graeco-Roman philosophy and religion, and critical post-Christian world views (liberalism, Marxism, romanticism).[29]

Ruether herself speaks of this combination of sources and critical principle as "practical eclecticism" or "feminist 'ecumenism.' " "This practical eclecticism indicates that . . . Jewish and Christian feminists stand on a boundary, facing two directions, and refuse to opt simply for one against the other."[30] The feminist theologian, regardless of her tradition of origin, draws on whatever sources and norms she needs to to promote the full humanity of women. "Thus, feminist theological reflection takes place in the context of a feminist 'ecumenism' between religious traditions that does not necessarily feel bound by the traditional Christian boundaries between true and false religion."[31] A feminist theology may or may not continue to define itself as Christian, depending on the extent to which it regards revelation through Jesus the Christ as normative.[32] Thus, a feminist theology that begins from Christian roots and uses Christian symbols may or may not continue to regard itself as a Christian theology.

We gain some insight into Ruether's suggestions for change when we look further at the nontraditional sources that she chooses for her theology. She looks to movements considered marginal or heretical by the Christian tradition but that preserve a vision of human equality, where women had roles of leadership and importance, and concludes that one of the reasons for their marginalization is, in fact, the place they gave women.

The usefulness of these movements is in the historical, alternative role models they may provide for women. We do not and cannot stand as though we had no history at all; we cannot begin anew, so to speak, for we are historically situated beings, influenced in the present by our past. If some of that past can be found to have been egalitarian for women, we might learn from it for the present. Ruether is not naïve about these traditions. She does not think that we can simply use, for example, Montanism in place of dominant Christian tradition, partly because our knowledge of it is fragmentary, partly because she recognizes that no historical tradition is totally immune to patriarchy, partly because she recognizes that there were historical and theological reasons (not all of them good, admittedly) why such traditions became marginal.

Ruether draws on pre-Christian "pagan" traditions because they are part of the historical background of Judaism and Christianity. Again, she is not naïve about their presenting a glowing alternative to patriarchal Christianity, but she does think that through them we might discover new insights into the beginnings of Judaism and Christianity.

There are three contemporary movements on which Ruether draws specifically: liberalism, romanticism, and Marxism. Again, she does not do this uncritically but with a view to the fact that these movements give feminists insight into the contemporary world, and thus provide certain perspectives essential to the kinds of criticism feminists are leveling at Christian theology. Feminists can use the best of the critical strands in each of these traditions in coming to a new feminist theological synthesis, taking a variety of influences on contemporary culture and religion into account.

According to Ruether, feminist theology must not be built on the foundation of Scripture, or tradition, or church, but on the belief in a divine foundation that is ultimately good, on a "primal re-encounter with divine reality."[33] This "new" foundation is not totally discontinuous with the past, for, as we can see from the list of sources Ruether consults, it builds on past foundations, and yet it reenvisions the Christian stories, it recasts and reinterprets these stories. Instructively, Ruether compares this move to the way in which Christians recast and reinterpreted the stories of the Hebrew people. She sees feminism as a "new midrash," a "third Covenant," a "new beginning."[34]

Because she sees the need to situate herself historically, not in a vacuum, and because of her own historical situation within the Christian tradition, Ruether sees the biblical liberating tradition as essential both to her Christian and to her feminist identity. Ruether does not want to abandon the tradition; she realizes that we must situate ourselves somehow or another with regard to our history, we must have some disposition toward what has gone before us. Neither, however, does she want to romanticize that tradition as if it could be taken on approvingly as it is and without question.

Her attitude toward what she sees as the liberating, prophetic tradition derived from Scripture appears to have changed somewhat over the years. Earlier in her career (until the publication of *Sexism and God-Talk*) she gave the liberating witness she finds in Scripture a more central place in her theologizing.[35] Now, although the Christian tradition is a central source for the symbols she uses and holds important in her theology, she finds less place for the normative value of these symbols in feminist theology. Dedication to feminist aims is more crucial to her theology than adherence to some particular criterion or standard of "Christian-ness." Nonetheless she thinks that Christianity as a religious tradition is vital as long as its revelatory pattern can be reproduced for each generation and as long as it continues to speak to individuals about the redemptive meaning of their experience.[36] What feminist theology does, then, for Ruether, is to correct the androcentrism of every category of Christianity.

According to Ruether, traditional theology needs to change because it has not promoted the full humanity of women. The scriptural texts and virtually all the other theological texts available in the Christian tradition are patriarchal texts. The symbols and stories from these texts do not serve to affirm women but rather to oppress them.

Women's experience, says Ruether, is never at the center of the traditional texts, women are not treated as active, thinking, experiencing subjects, and therefore, new texts need to be found and used so that women's experience can be made visible.

> [Canonical patriarchal texts] lose their normative status and we read them critically in the light of that larger reality that they hide and deny. In the process, a new norm emerges on which to

construct a new community, a new theology, eventually a new canon. That new norm makes women as subjects the center rather than the margin. Women are empowered to define themselves rather than be defined by others. Women's speech and presence are normative rather than aberrant.[37]

The women's experience that needs to be taken into account includes their experience of patriarchy and the ways it has limited both women and men and kept both from developing to their full potential in one way or another. Ruether also notes that even the one type of experience that women have always been able to claim as their own, the biological experiences of menstruation, birthing, suckling, and the like, have hitherto been interpreted through patriarchal eyes. Therefore, even these bodily experiences have to be reinterpreted and used in ways that women can recognize as their own.[38] Women need to claim the right to write their own texts and create their own stories out of their religious experiences, rather than being told by others (men) what those texts and symbols and stories should be.

Women do not have time to wait for the patriarchal church to reform before they can take part in meaningful worship; they also need to build alternative communities of worship where they can use the texts and symbols and stories that speak to them. Ruether, like many others, speaks of this alternative community as "women-church."[39]

While she emphasizes the need to take account of the full humanity of women, Ruether has always been careful in her theology not to emphasize this full humanity of women at the expense of other groups of human beings or at the expense of the nonhuman world. She has always recognized the weblike interconnection of oppressions and the fact that working specifically to eradicate the oppression of one group must always take into account the oppressions of others. She truly believes that none are free until all are free, and her work has often dealt with other oppressions, and the recognition of how, for example, racism, sexism, and the exploitation of nature are all linked to the same attitude of dominance over the subordinate.

Although it is feminist readings of the Bible that discern what the norm for theology and for understanding and criticizing Scripture should be, the Bible does contain material useful to women in what Ruether calls the "prophetic-liberating" or the "prophetic-messianic" traditions. "I identify myself as a Christian in terms of what I would call the 'prophetic-messianic core' of biblical faith. This I see as the norm for judging both Scripture and tradition."[40] To the extent that the Bible reflects this prophetic, liberating message, it can be seen to be authoritative for feminist theology because this message can be used to promote the full humanity of women.

When feminism claims the prophetic-liberating tradition as a norm, it does not choose a trend or a tradition marginal to the biblical witness, "it chooses a tradition that can be fairly claimed, on the basis of generally accepted Biblical scholarship, to be the central tradition, the tradition by which Biblical faith constantly criticizes and renews itself and its own vision."[41]

This prophetic-liberating tradition in the Bible takes the side of those who are disadvantaged or oppressed. This is the tradition, both in the Hebrew Bible and in the Christian New Testament, that challenges the status quo, criticizes social oppression, exposes the corruption of false religion, and calls for repentance. The exodus is the fundamental biblical symbol for this prophetic-liberating tradition, but it is carried on by the prophets and by Jesus. The salvation sought and offered in this central tradition is an alternative future, a new society of peace and justice where there are no oppressors and no oppressed.[42] God in this tradition is the one who denounces the oppressors and defends the oppressed. All religiosity that serves to sanctify injustice is criticized and found wanting.

The prophetic-liberating tradition in the Bible takes different forms according to the situations in which it arises. Different criticisms and reforms are suited to different times and places.

This critical principle derived from the Bible is the norm by which the rest of the biblical witness is to be judged. Traditions within Scripture that seem to permit or condone the status quo of oppressors and oppressed are not acceptable as authoritative.

According to Ruether, Jesus continues in the prophetic-messianic tradition. As she noted in 1981, "One's portrait of Jesus ultimately expresses one's normative statement about the Christian message to the world today."[43] Although she would place less normative weight on Jesus today, a given portrait of him is still important for her as a theological source. He is a political figure who defends the lowly and judges the mighty. He models a leadership based on service to others, and he expects his followers to act in the same way, so that the result can be mutual empowerment. To paint him as an apolitical figure would justify and sustain the status quo rather than challenge it.[44] In his political action, in his defense of the oppressed, he radicalizes the view of God's reign that was current at his time.

Jesus' maleness is not central to his importance. What is central is his message, his judgment on all that excludes or subordinates some people and raises others to pride of place. Jesus' relationship to God is one of mutual love and care, not one where God appears as despot or tyrant. Therefore, not even this relationship can be used to justify dominance and subordination. His relationships to women and the roles they play as his followers show their importance in receiving and spreading the good news. "Once the mythology about Jesus as Messiah or divine *Logos*, with its traditional masculine imagery, is stripped off, the Jesus of the synoptic Gospels can be recognized as a figure remarkably compatible with feminism."[45]

This quotation points to another central point in Ruether's christology. She sees Jesus as pointing beyond himself to the one who is to come, and she does not, therefore, see him as final, even for Christianity. Jesus announced the messianic hope and gave signs of its presence, but the final point of messianic advent is not in his present but in the future.

Ruether distinguishes in her theology between Jesus, the historical figure who points beyond himself, and the Christ, "the messianic humanity" who is disclosed to us in many times and places, Jesus included.[46] She worries about attributing finality to any historical figure because she thinks this discounts its historicity and makes the Christ into a timeless revelation that is closed and to which access can only be had through the apostolic teachings. Ruether thinks that Jesus is one place where Christ is disclosed to us, but she also thinks that this humanity continues to be disclosed to us in our sisters and brothers.

In addition, Ruether fears that attributing finality to Jesus will breed anti-Semitism by totally discounting the validity of Judaism. She also thinks that any emphasis on the finality of Christ in Jesus leaves no more room for the inspiration of the Holy Spirit, no room for us to hear God speaking to us in the present.

For her, true church is the community of liberation from oppression, a community where the Spirit rules and where patriarchy is no more. "The Church is where the good news of liberation from sexism is preached, where the Spirit is present to empower us to renounce patriarchy, where a community committed to the new life of mutuality is gathered together and nurtured, and where the community is spreading this vision and struggle to others."[47]

Today Ruether sees a need for women-church, a stage in *ekklesia* where women claim the right to be church, where they claim the exodus tradition as the tradition of liberation from patriarchy and where they reject the notion that patriarchy is God's will. Women-church allows women to be the church empowered by the Spirit without waiting interminably for the institutional church as a whole to recognize women's rightful claim to equal status.

Norms from Christian Tradition

Letty Russell is a good example of a feminist theologian who draws norms for Christian theology both explicitly from Christian tradition and from women's experience.[48] In contrast to Schüssler Fiorenza and Ruether, Letty Russell is a Protestant. Much of her writing has centered around the issue of theology as a shared enterprise rather than as the enterprise of isolated individuals. She sees her feminist theology in continuity with the other theologies of liberation. For her, theology is not just thought, for it flows out of and into action. She speaks of theology, Christian theology, as using one's *logos* (mind) "in the perspective of God, as God is known in and through the Word in the world."[49] At times she even equates theology and praxis.[50] One seeks to know and understand God, and thereby to know and understand oneself and others. As a Christian theological task, this is not just an understanding of one's own present experience or the present experiences of others, but must be carefully and consciously related to the Christian tradition, "the accumulated action-reflection of the 'communion of saints.' "[51] The purpose of theology is not only, or even primarily, better understanding, but action, change. One's understanding of the Word in the world propels one to action consonant with that Word.

We are historical beings who do not and cannot merely mimic unquestioningly and unthinkingly what our ancestors have said, in matters of faith as in other matters. As comforting as it might be to some to think that one might be able to come up with the definitive Christian theology for all times and places, the fact is that as situations change questions (and answers) change too. Looking back over the history of Christian theology, we can discern how different contexts yielded different emphases. Our job is to discern in our time and place what it means to be the children of God.[52] "Christian community has a pattern of criteria for what is an authoritative witness to God in Jesus

Christ. Usually that configuration includes the resources of scientific knowledge and human experience as well as those of
scripture and church tradition."[53]

For Russell (as for other feminist theologians) the need to
rethink theology has been prompted by the recognition of women
as an oppressed group. Because theology has traditionally been
done by men, women's history has not been included in the
recounting of the history of Christianity. If women were to ask
and answer theological questions, how would theology change?

Russell says, "The importance of women doing theology is
the same as that of any other group around the world. They
make a contribution to the *unfinished dimension* of theology."[54]
She is not claiming that feminist theology is the final and static
word either. "No one person writing theology out of a particular
set of life experiences can interpret the meaning of the gospel
for all others."[55] Theology is an ongoing activity, not a final end
in itself.

Yet it is clear that for Russell, experience, and in particular,
women's experience, has a bearing on Christian theology. Indeed, experience is one of the norms of judging the adequacy
or truthfulness of religious tradition. No theology is adequate if
it cannot speak to and from the experience of its participants,
its doers and hearers. "Women's experience" includes the biological and cultural experiences of being female as well as the
feminist experience, the political experience of those who ad-
vocate a "change of society to include both women and men as
human beings."[56] All of these should inform an adequate Christian theology, where diversity of experience is acknowledged
and welcomed.

The normative importance of women's experience has had
many implications for the way Russell theologizes, for, as she
rightly sees, feminist theology is a "paradigm shift" in theology
that brings into question "what has been understood as authoritative in every aspect of biblical religion."[57] What needs to
be challenged, then, is everything in our Christian past and

present that seeks to limit woman's full humanity, full acceptance as an equal.[58] "No interpretation of authority that reinforces patriarchal structures of domination would be acceptable for feminist interpretation."[59]

One of the challenges raised by this paradigm shift is the challenge to what Russell speaks of as an "unusable" past.[60] A past that is not usable is a past that has been and is used in the present to argue or act against the full humanity of women. One seeks, instead, a "usable past," the parts of our history where women have been recognized as full and equal human beings. In the search for a usable past, one does not deny incidents of the past, but one approaches them with new questions in order to prevent them from continuing as instruments of oppression. If one does not look critically at one's past, it may serve to function as a (perhaps unconscious) force determining one's present. One asks about who recorded this past and why. One looks for the past of women, a hidden past that has not been considered important until recently.

Another challenge raised by recognizing the importance of women's experience is the search for a "usable language." Like many other feminists, Russell has long recognized that women have often been made invisible not only by the record of historical events, but also in the way we have traditionally supposed male terms to be generic.

Her search for a usable language also includes a search for the "forgotten names of God" and for new ways to speak of God to supplement the traditional male language.[61] "The metaphors we use are powerful God-talk, for they determine the way we think about God and about ourselves as men and women, created in God's image."[62]

Language is not just a tool. Like the past, our language too can exercise power over us or we over it. "Power determines the way language is used, because those who are able to carry out their intent do so in regard to human communication as well as other matters."[63]

A third challenge that women's experience presents to traditional theologizing, one for which Russell is probably best known, is the challenge to individualism in theology. She prefers instead a method that emphasizes the corporate nature of humanity and encourages what she calls "partnership."

> The emerging feminist paradigm trying to make sense of biblical and theological truth claims is that of *authority as partnership*. In this view, reality is interpreted in the form of a circle of interdependence. Ordering is explored through inclusion of diversity in a rainbow spectrum that does not require that persons submit to the "top" but, rather, that they participate in the common task of creating an interdependent community of humanity and nature. Authority is exercised *in* community and tends to reinforce ideas of cooperation, with contributions from a wide diversity of persons enriching the whole.[64]

This notion is not one of hierarchical authority but of shared authority. It seeks a "more inclusive consensus on theological issues" and recognizes the value of a variety of opinions and points of view.[65] If a variety of points of view is represented, one can challenge and question rather than simply accept a given point of view of a particular authority. Partnership recognizes all people as subjects, not objects, it lauds interdependence rather than independence.

From her perspective as a feminist, Russell thinks that the Word of God heard in Scripture and tradition needs to be liberated from its androcentrism and from privatized and spiritualized interpretation. But here we must turn to Russell's understanding of how Christian tradition functions in theology, for although she raises questions about the androcentrism of the Christian tradition from her experiences as a woman, she also raises them from her commitment as a Christian.

Russell derives her central theological norm from the Christian tradition itself. "In the Christian faith there is a *center* (commitment to Jesus christ [*sic*]) and a *circle* (a hermeneutical circle). Every theological interpretation affects every other, so that we continue to move around the circle trying to create models and images that are faithful to the center of our commitment."[66] A Christian theologian "cannot abandon the story of Jesus of Nazareth."[67] One cannot get away from the center, Jesus Christ, and still do Christian theology.

It is on the basis of her understanding of the significance of Jesus and the way that is expressed in Scripture that Russell understands what makes the Christian tradition *Christian*. She speaks of "the self-revelation of God in Jesus Christ and through the Spirit" not as itself the authority, but as the *source* of authority in our lives as Christians.[68] We note that God's self-revelation in Jesus is central to this understanding of authority, but it is not its only element; God's self-revelation in the Spirit is also important.

Russell sees the importance of Jesus as an importance of example. "He came to human beings where they were and sat where they sat, and out of that spoke to their inmost being."[69] Jesus was the inaugurator of God's kingdom. He healed and taught. Russell speaks of Jesus as the representative of true humanity and God; as God's entering into history to be with human beings. Jesus calls us also to be true humans and to live out our true humanity in working for liberation. "In Jesus Christ, God addresses us and provides a living relationship to help us shape the present and future of our lives."[70] Through Jesus' actions, we learn what is demanded of us.

Russell sees in the actions of Jesus the occasion to question many of the structures and systems of which her own experience has led her to be suspicious; for instance, she sees Jesus' actions as showing that permanent hierarchy is not a necessity of existence. No one person or one group should be permanently dominant over or subordinate to others.

The good news about Jesus Christ is conveyed to the church through the Scriptures. Russell maintains that we must be wary, however, about taking the whole of the Bible as Word of God. In the Gospels we get the story of God's love active in the world in Jesus Christ, yet how we hear that gospel message depends on who we are and where we are.

For Russell, "Word of God" is not something written, it is something experienced when the written word addresses the hearer in a way that she or he can hear it as good news. To help make this clear she distinguishes between Scripture and Script. Scripture is the written record as we have it, Script is the way it speaks to us and becomes the Word of God in our lives.[71]

Russell expresses the key that she uses to unlock the Word of God from Scripture in several ways. Sometimes she centers her remarks on Jesus.

> For me the importance of tradition is found . . . in the significance of . . . *Tradition as the dynamic relationship of God with us* in handing over Jesus Christ into the hands of all generations and nations. It is this relationship with Christ that provides a key for me to the authority of both Scripture and Church tradition. In the light of this key I ask how to relate in trust and faithfulness to God and others as we seek to decide what to do as believers in Jesus Christ and members of the community of people who long for and live out God's hoped for promise of new wholeness and human community.[72]

This quotation focuses on one aspect of the past as a key to the past, present, and future. One looks to Jesus Christ to know how we as believers must act, and he provides the normative focus. Yet, also in this quotation, we see a future emphasis, an emphasis that becomes clearer in some of Russell's other statements about her interpretive key. "The particular interpretive key that assists me in continuing to give assent is the witness of scripture to God's promise (for the mending of creation) on its way to fulfilment. That which denies this intention of God for the liberation of groaning creation in all its parts does not compel or evoke my assent."[73] This description of her interpretive key also refers back to Scripture. Although she does not explicitly refer to Jesus Christ in this statement, it is clear that she sees his message as proclaiming the future mending of creation as God's goal and God's promise. Here her reference is pointed more toward the future, which is a very important theological category for Russell.

Her interest in the future is piqued first, I think, by the desire for things to be different from the way they are now. So one might well say that this interest is derived from her experience as a woman and as a witness to the oppression of others, longing for a world where it is not so. But her understanding of the future as theologically important derives from her understanding of God's Word in Scripture.

In Jesus Christ Russell sees the announcement of a possible and promised future, a time of justice, freedom, and wholeness. In Jesus Christ God's new creation is begun. And the promise of this new creation enables us to interpret other biblical and traditional texts.

> Interpreting the Bible from a critical perspective of God's promised future leads us to begin from the other end and to engage in what might be called eschatological hermeneutics, a process of questioning our actions and our society in the light of the biblical message of New Creation. We begin with *questions* that arise out of our life and out of the experience of those who cry for deliverance; not simply with those of the "non-believer" but with those of the "non-person." These questions are addressed critically to the tradition of the Christian faith and to the Bible as the chief witness to God's promise in Jesus Christ. The *biblical message*, in turn, helps us to interpret itself, for a central motif of the Bible . . . is that of "promise on the way to fulfilment."[74]

Christians are called to work toward the new creation, following Jesus' example and catching glimpses of what that New Creation is from Jesus and from other biblical stories of liberation. According to Russell, there are no final principles by which to make our theological judgments, only clues along the way, for even though we can see the centrality of Jesus, Christians are called "to live out the story of Jesus Christ in ever-new circumstances. When a person and not a principle is at the center of our life the relationship itself is never static. This means that the meaning of God's intention for creation and the image of God cannot be described in static terms."[75]

Christians remember the past and move toward the future in hope, knowing that they move toward God's new creation. This new creation is a wholistic creation where each human being is valued by all others, where class and gender are not categories of domination and subordination. It is in light of this theme of new creation that Russell sees liberation and universality as two major biblical motifs, and thus sees biblical stories embodying these motifs as of utmost importance to understanding God's relationship to the world.

Because women cannot appeal to a past of equality and respect, it is helpful for them to be able to envisage a different, nonpatriarchal future and to appeal to that as authority instead. "Biblical theology itself is 'hope filled' and provides images of jubilee and liberation, images of promise on the way to fulfilment. Thus our memory of the future becomes an appeal to the future of the oppressed, the marginal, the 'little ones' of God's *oikos* (household), for whom the scriptures hold out a vision of new society."[76]

Russell recognizes that much of the Bible is patriarchal and hence refuses to identify the Word of God with the Bible. Yet she does not want to abandon the biblical witness, because "it makes sense of [her] experience and speaks to [her] about the meaning and purpose of [her] humanity in Jesus Christ."[77] As long as the biblical witness continues to speak to her about the basic questions of life, she will continue to listen.

She sees her use of Scripture in continuity with the criteria David Kelsey sets out as the limits of authoritative Christian interpretation of Scripture. "The claim must include intelligible discourse capable of consistent formulation and reasoned elaboration and justification; it must reflect the structure of tradition as scripture is used to nurture and reform the identity of a particular faith community; and it must be seriously imaginable in the particular cultural context where the interpretation takes place."[78] Nonetheless, she is quite clear that Scripture cannot be the only authority for Christian community or Christian theology. "In the perspective of authority in community, the interpretive key is no longer one external or one internal biblical key but rather a configuration of sources of faith that seek to enrich the way God might be present with us."[79]

There are many models for methodology in feminist theology. The three explicated here express three different emphases in understanding the interaction between Christian tradition and women's experience. In the remainder of the book, in dialogue with the three emphases represented here, I will explore further the themes of women's experience and authoritative tradition with a view to gaining some clarity in the use of the terms and presenting their relationship in the particular theological method espoused here.

3/
WOMEN'S EXPERIENCE AS SOURCE AND NORM OF THEOLOGY

The feminist consensus outlined in chapter 1 is confirmed in chapter 2 when one considers the areas of agreement shared by Schüssler Fiorenza, Ruether, and Russell. And the consensus clearly centers around the need to make use of present experience, in particular, women's experience, in one's theology. This said, however, there is still a need to try to define what is meant by the term "women's experience," for the term is used more often than it is defined.[1] What I propose to do in this chapter is to synthesize the many ways in which the term "women's experience" has been used and to discuss how women's experience so understood might function as source and norm of feminist theology.

"Women's experience" is the multiplicity of things women experience, both individually and as a group. But this is a very broad definition. How can it be understood in such a way that it is of some use in theology?

The first thing to be said in this connection is that when we speak of women's experience, we are talking first and foremost of experience as reflected upon, what might be called knowledge, rather than immediate experience. Alfred North Whitehead has argued that both knowledge and sense experience are derivative and dependent forms of the human being's dealings with the world. The primary relationship of the human being to the world is that of the human being as experiencing subject, where the term "experience" denotes first and foremost the basic experience of being a self in relation to the whole of reality of which one is a part and in relation to others within that whole.

> What is our primary experience which lies below and gives its meaning to our conscious analysis of qualitative detail? In our analysis of detail we are presupposing a background which supplies a meaning. These vivid accents accentuate something which is already there. We require to describe that factor in our experience which, being a matter of course, does not enter prominently into conversation. There is no need to mention it. For this reason language is very ineffective for the exposition of metaphysics.
>
> Our enjoyment of actuality is a realization of worth, good or bad. It is a value experience. Its basic expression is—Have a care, here is something that matters! Yes—that is the best phrase—the primary glimmering of consciousness reveals, something that matters.
>
> This experience provokes attention, dim and, all but, subconscious. Attention yields a three-fold character in the "Something that matters.". "Totality," "Externality," and "Internality" are the primary characterizations of "that which matters." They are not to be conceived as clear, analytic concepts. Experience awakes them with dim detailed analysis. They are presuppositions in the sense of expressing the sort of obviousness which experience exhibits. There is the totality of actual fact; there is the externality of many facts; there is the internality of this experiencing which lies within the totality.[2]

Knowledge and sense experience are dependent on that primary experience that underlies and supports them. Clear and distinct consciousness arises out of this primary experience which Whitehead calls nonsensuous perception. What Whitehead has given expression to here is our awareness that we do have an experience more primary and basic than the intellectual experience that is knowledge. Our sense experience and our reflection require that we abstract details from the whole and focus on these. We do not, however, *first* perceive or focus on abstractions or details that we then put together in order to have an impression of the whole. Rather, from an impression of the whole we gradually abstract and focus on the details. We are aware, for instance, when we enter a new place for the first time, that we have a sense of the place, a dim sense of our surroundings before we discern any of its details. Even when we are asleep, when our senses are not making things clear and distinct for us, we are experiencing that which is around us. We do not experience our bodies through our senses but through our non-sensuous perception, and we experience our own immediate past in the same way.

This nonsensuous experience is also experience of God, because God, in order to be worthy of that name at all, must be universal, and thus, all that exists must be universally related to God. If God is universal, any experience at all includes experience of God. God, as universal, is present to the world as its foundation and goal. This original experience, however, is not an experience of God where God is consciously recognized *as God*, for such an experience of God is not simply immediate experience but also involves reflection on that immediate experience. Thus, to talk of what we experience as God or to call that God by male names is a product not of immediate experience but of reflection on that experience.

The experience we have, whatever "the externality of many facts," is filtered, interpreted through the lens of who we are, reflected upon in light of "the internality of this experiencing," what our cumulative experience of the past has made us. I do think that one can argue for certain universal human experiences of longing for meaning and purpose, of hoping that what we do is significant, of trust that, in balance, life is worth living and has ultimate purpose, and I will make this point below. But whatever these experiences in their immediacy, the articulation and understanding of them change as factors such as culture, gender, race, and class, mold one's expectations and reflections.

Even those who posit a universal human experience of transcendence (as I do), of what Christians call God, know that the
way this experience gets articulated depends on a host of factors,
both communal and individual.

Of course, it is not only our interpretations of experience
that differ; the content of experience, except for its most basic
metaphysical underpinnings, varies too; we do not all experience
the same things. Here we are interested in the difference between
men's experience and women's experience. Men and women
have different experience. Even when they are party to the same
event, they might well experience and interpret it differently. The
point of focusing on women's experience is to articulate and
reflect upon it further. Here, too, when I speak of women's experience, I speak from the perspective of a white, middle-class,
Western woman. Women's experience may be seen differently
from other perspectives. I am trying, however, to offer a fairly
broad description and interpretation of the term, hoping thereby
to be more than merely idiosyncratic.

So, what are we discussing when we discuss women's experience? Of course, there are numerous factors involved in how
one experiences something and how one interprets that experience. In talking about women's experience I do not want to
claim that men do not or cannot have some of these same
experiences or that they can never interpret them the way women
do. Nor do I claim that women's experience as women is so
totally abstractable from the rest of women's experience as human that one can isolate and dissect it as one can a laboratory
experiment.

Nonetheless, we do, after all, experience our world as gen-
dered beings, so we cannot easily pass over how experience
might differ when we talk of women's experience and men's
experience. I am convinced by the feminist claim that because
traditional Christian theology is the product of male hands,
hearts, and minds, we should look beyond it to see if and how

women might draw on their experiences to do theology differently.

In this section of the chapter I will detail five ways of talking about women's experience. I will speak of women's bodily experience, women's socialized experience (what culture teaches us about being women), women's feminist experience (response to women's socialized experience), women's historical experience, and women's individual experiences. In later sections I will ask how such experience might be seen to be source and norm of Christian feminist theology.

Many feminists talk about women's bodily experience. What difference does it make to live "in" a woman's body? Is the world experienced differently, and, if so, how? Here we need to differentiate further between the biological experiences women have, as Whitehead says, the nonsensuous way in which we relate to our bodies, and the socialized reactions to these bodily experiences, especially those encouraged and fostered by the Western world.

All women menstruate or have menstruated; we all have some measure of sexual experience, however varied; most women experience pregnancy and childbirth; many of us live to experience menopause. Some women, reflecting on these biological experiences of womanhood, have argued that women with their cyclical relationship to their bodies are closer to nature, more aligned to the pulls and powers of the earth. Penelope Washbourn sees the opportunity for graceful or demonic resolution of the crisis caused by each of the biological stages of a woman's life.[3] Others have argued that if there is a difference between men's and women's closeness to nature, it is a learned difference, or that such a difference is only imaginary.

Clearly, we are taught socialized reactions to our bodily experience. For young girls, the fear of pregnancy, of its biological and social consequences, conditions their reactions to their bodies. For an increasing number of women approaching middle age, the fear of not becoming pregnant, of infertility, also colors how they experience their bodies and themselves for society has taught them to believe they have failed, they are not "real" women.

In our society there is also the very real sense of vulnerability as women fear being raped or assaulted; or a woman's sense of betrayal and violation when she has been raped or assaulted. Another factor in woman's bodily experience is body image; first that her body is her most important asset and second that her body will never measure up to the ideal society has imposed. All these bodily factors have to be considered when we speak of the place of women's experience in theology.

When I speak of women's socialized experience, I mean what the culture teaches us about being women. This socialized experience of what it means to be a woman has been largely male defined; males, as Mary Daly rightly noted, took upon themselves the power of "naming" and prevented women from doing the same.[4]

The result that this has had on our images of women has been well documented in psychological, sociological, historical, and theological literature.[5] The image of woman that we in the twentieth-century Western world have been socialized to accept is the image of woman as less important than man, the one whose sphere is home and family and whose whole worth is tied up in the bearing and raising of children. By contrast, man's sphere is the sphere of work, the sphere of money, the sphere of the "real world." Woman, because of this emphasis on her childbearing role, is associated with body and not mind and has been considered of feebler intellect.

The notion that the world of work was the "real world" also contributed to women's marginalization. Even though lip service was paid to the importance of childbearing and child rearing, little value was placed on this role in economic terms, and this led to little value being placed on it in social terms as well.

Women have been taught to respect and adhere to the "virtues" of meekness, obedience, and self-denial. We have been taught that aggression does not become a "lady."[6] Women, we have been taught, should be nurturers, helpers, supporters of their mates and children; they should expect to be taken care of financially in return for taking care of the realms of morals and emotional support.

Women's feminist experience is a response to women's socialized experience. This socialized experience, being (and seeing the world) dominated and controlled by men, often served and still serves to exclude women from jobs and financial security, from pursuing their interests and talents, from making genuine choices about their lives from a broad range of options. Were men really more suited to political and social power than women? Were women intrinsically more suited to child rearing than men?

Women began to realize that they themselves needed to articulate their experience rather than accept a male definition of what it should be. They realized that they had to ask themselves what women were like and what they truly wanted. They needed to claim the power of naming for themselves. They needed to ask for equality with men and to ask just what equality might mean. Wherein were their similarities? Wherein were their differences? What effects should these similarities and differences have on economic and social power and value?

Women began to ask what it meant to be whole human beings, unrestricted by stereotyped roles of gender identity and to seek wholeness for themselves and others. They also reflected on the fact that so many women were poor, and asked why this should be and how it could be changed. They considered how race or class status affected women's roles and expectations.

Women's feminist experience is the experience of questioning all that we have been told about being women. It is the experience of refusing to take at face value anyone's definition of what it means to be a woman. It is the experience of redefining what "woman" means by redefining whose experience counts as valuable.

Another category of women's experience might be called women's historical experience, not experience that we have directly for ourselves but what we know and can learn of the women who have gone before us. It may by now be a cliché that those who do not know their past are doomed to repeat it, but women often have not known their past. This has been so for a number of reasons. Women and their lives have been excluded from most history books; if they have been included at all, it is as caricatures. Feminist historians are discovering, however, that they can recover some of the lost history of women, and we need to and can draw on the experience of these women.

Finally, women's experience is the myriads of individual experiences each woman has in her lifetime. Some of these might be fitted into the categories above, but it is important to keep reminding ourselves that experience can only be generalized so far. Nonetheless these individual experiences can act as catalysts for theological reflection.

Judith Plaskow summarizes her view of women's experience in a way that serves well here: " 'Women's experience' means simply this: the experience of women in the course of a history never free from cultural role definitions."[7]

Women's Experience as a Source
for Theology

Women's feminist experience gives us the key to the use of women's experience in theology, for it is women's feminist experience that causes us to begin to question. Not only in society but in theology women began to question the definitions of womanhood. Who made these definitions, and were they valid? Could women recognize themselves?

The feminist theological consensus outlined in chapter 1 details many of the ways in which women saw that they were not included in theology. However much the supposedly generic "man" was used in theology, women were not its intended audience and were its subjects only as deviant or as caricature. Then the question had to be asked, How would theology be different if women were its subjects and its audience? What would it mean in theology to take women's experience seriously?

To answer this question we must begin by defining the term "theology." In general, liberation theology speaks of theology first as action and only secondarily as reflection.[8] Such an understanding implies that one first "does" theology by engaging in liberating praxis, and that reflection on that praxis, although necessary for theology, is secondary to commitment to liberating praxis. I realize that such a definition of theology arises for some good reasons. Theology has often been used as a substitute for Christian action or a buttress for the status quo, a refusal to see the need for change. Yet misuse of theology does not necessarily mean that the traditional definition itself is faulty.

The Christian must be about the work of liberation in the world. At this point, I am in full accord with liberation theology's self-understanding. My misgiving about equating theology and liberating praxis takes shape because this equation gives rise to the possibility of activity that forgets its Christian roots. We only know what *Christian* praxis is by reflecting on what Christian witness is. Such activity may be to the benefit of humanity and that is important and good, but I am not sure that it is a sufficient starting point for Christian theology.

I think of theology primarily as reflective (as befits its derivation from *logos* about *theos*, words or reasoning about God), and I make a distinction between leading a Christian life and Christian theology, the serious and critical reflection that leads to full understanding of what the Christian faith is and what Christian activity can and should be. I make this distinction because, although I do think that a committed Christian faith requires one to act for the liberation of all God's creatures, I think that it takes some level of reflection, of theologizing, to make this clear. Although theology might well inspire liberating action in the world, and indeed ought to inspire such action in Christian adherents, theology *is not itself* this action. I also draw this distinction to make it evident that one does not have to be a Christian or to consider oneself a Christian in order to engage in or understand Christian theology. Those who equate Christian theology and Christian practice exclude all those who do not call themselves Christian, do not engage in Christian practice, from understanding Christian theology.

Nor is theology, if reflective, reflection only on liberating praxis. One might engage in liberating praxis and subsequently reflect on it, but unless one reflects on that praxis one does not know whether or not it is Christian praxis, praxis in line with the Christian witness of faith. And one does not know that the praxis is in line with the Christian witness of faith unless one has reflected not just on one's liberating activity but as fully as possible on the totality of that witness. When I use the term "Christian witness of faith" I mean by it any understanding, articulating, and living out of what Christianity is and what it entails. It is not necessarily at every point fully critical and fully reflective.[9]

The task of Christian theology is the fully reflective and fully critical task of helping individuals, whether Christian or not, to understand and articulate the Christian witness of faith adequately for their own time and place. It presupposes the existence of a cumulative tradition of Christian witness as the object of its reflections, and it reflects critically on that received Christian witness in order to understand its meaning, to evaluate its claims to truth, to see how it has been used in the past to foster or hinder fulness of human life, and, in that process, to decide how the Christian faith should be expressed in word and deed for one's time and place.

Christian theology deals with two central "givens." The received Christian witness, that is, what the Christian tradition has been in the past, is the first of these; and the situation today, in the time and the place this Christian theology is articulated, is the second.[10]

Any Christian theology must, first and foremost, attempt to articulate the *Christian* faith as it understands that term. Otherwise the adjective "Christian" is meaningless. But it must also articulate that witness for its situation; otherwise the whole theology is meaningless for its intended audience. This second task may, of course, require a reconception of the Christian witness of faith. That will be one of the main concerns of the next chapter. In this chapter I am specifically concerned with the ways in which theology should speak to its own time and place.

Like Schüssler Fiorenza, Ruether, and Russell, I do not think that there is any neutral, objective place one can stand to do one's theologizing. One must be willing to articulate the starting point for one's theology rather than claiming to stand outside all commitments. What one must be prepared to do, then, is to argue for the suitability of one's own starting point and to demonstrate the adequacy of a position developed from it.

My own starting point is a feminist one. I am a feminist because of my conviction, based on my personal experience and on the recounted experiences (both historical and contemporary) of other women, that women have been systematically oppressed. This systematic oppression has stereotyped women in a variety of ways and has kept them under male control, both socially and politically. I maintain an explicitly feminist theology, which means that one of its main goals is to avoid contributing to women's continued oppression, to promote the full humanity of women rather than stifle it.

Although this theology is explicitly feminist, thereby focusing its areas of concern, its goal is to speak to a broader audience, not merely to converted feminists. All theology is written from some stance or other, but theology also makes claims to be more generally understandable and persuasive to those who do not begin by sharing its point of view. Moreover, although this theology has a feminist stance, it does not argue this is the only legitimate stance from which to begin. Indeed, this theology in no way wants to discount other forms of oppression that may provide the beginning points for other theologies. This theology will have succeeded if, in its particularity, it also speaks to the general questions any theology must raise and answer.

A Christian feminist theology tries to articulate adequately the Christian witness of faith from the perspective of women as an oppressed group.

How, then, with theology defined as I have defined it, can women's experience be a source of theology? In the first chapter I spoke of "source" as any element that enters into the formulation of one's theology. If this is what "source" is, any of the elements defined under "women's experience" could conceivably be used as source material for theology. One might appeal to women's bodily experience for a new angle of perception. Women's bodily experience might also be one source of new theological vocabulary for the twentieth century in the same way that, as Eleanor McLaughlin argues, it was a source of theological vocabulary in the Middle Ages, vocabulary that spoke of Mother Jesus nourishing us at her breasts or the infant Jesus being nursed at the breast of the supplicant.[11] Some would also argue that drawing on women's bodily experience of closeness to nature would give rise to a theology more in tune with the natural world, less inclined to place human beings above it, more inclined to see human beings as part of an interconnected whole.

From women's socialized experience we learn the traditional Christian virtues and from women's feminist experience we learn to question whether in fact women in our time and our place need to be called to these virtues. From women's socialized experience we learn how others have defined us; from women's feminist experience we begin to define ourselves. Women's socialized experience may be a good place for *men* to learn about themselves and their role as makers and definers of the theologically important. They may also learn from women's socialized experience the virtues they ought to cultivate.

Women's feminist experience is, for theology, the source of questioning the status quo. It challenges all assumptions by asking whether or not women have been included in any given theological formulation; by being included in any vision of anthropology, by being consulted, by being its authors or intended audience. It points to women's socialized experience as the product of learned behaviors on the part of both men and women. It insists that the doctrine of "man" be renamed and reconceived truly to include woman, not just as an afterthought but as one-half the concern. It is women's feminist experience that pronounces traditional theology to be in large part *incredible* for contemporary women (see the next section).

The experience of women past is certainly good source material for theology in the present. When women have thought and written theologically in the past, how has that changed theology? This means we need to look seriously at the past assuming that women thought theologically, no matter how difficult it may be in some cases to find written texts. We might find useful the experience they draw on, the language they use. How have the ways in which women have been constricted and restricted affected their theologizing? How has this constriction and restriction affected theology about women? What can we learn from their experience that might be useful for ours? Women of strength and purpose from any age can be a source of inspiration in ours.

We draw on the experience of women in the past for our theology in the same way that we draw on any past tradition in the church. We need to be open, however, to the possibility of drawing our source material—images, language, concepts—from sources more wide-ranging than the traditions of orthodox Christianity. There may well be marginal Christian sources or pre- or extra-Christian sources that prove important to new understandings of Christian theology.[12]

A concern with women's historical experience adds women's history to patriarchal history. It provides new models, new questions, and new evidence for theology.

Even though women's experience has been understood through broad categories here, we should not lose sight of the fact that although, as women, we share certain experiences, we cannot reduce the whole of our experience to common denominators. The history of Christian theology is full of innovators, people who took the received tradition and through brilliant insights of their own formulated theologies appropriate to their times and places. And a woman can and should draw on her own experience in the same way to give a new twist, a new angle, to ask a new question arising out of something that has happened to her.

As I hope I have made clear here, the sources of one's theology can be and are many and varied. Conceivably almost anything might act as source material for theology. Here, of course, I have been concentrating on how women's experience might be source for Christian theology. In the next chapter I will concentrate more specifically on source material from *within* the Christian tradition, on Scripture and subsequent Christian history.

Women's Experience as Norm

The question of women's experience is raised because women do not find much of contemporary theology *credible*. Rather than finding Christian theology liberating, many women have experienced only or mainly oppression from it. In Christian theology many women have been, in the terms of the liberation theologians, non-persons. In theology there have been many other non-persons, too, made so by class or race or geographical factors, and I do not want to disregard their oppression. But my central interest here is the experience that women have had as non-persons in the face of a Christian theology that talks neither to nor for them. Women are asking why they should believe or adhere to a theological point of view that either fosters women's second-class status or, at the very least, is content to permit that second-class status as the norm.

Any theology that expects to win adherents must be credible, it must be able to sustain questions and objections that might be raised. For theology to claim, as Christian theology has sometimes done, that it has its own standards and does not need to be reasonable by the world's standards is really to evade the difficult question of why then anybody outside the tradition should be expected to believe that it contains any truth whatsoever.

Christianity claims to be true not just for Christians but in general. If it is to sustain this claim, it must submit itself to scrutiny. I suggest that in terms of credibility, this scrutiny takes place on two main fronts.[13] First, are the theological claims and statements being made *intellectually* credible? Are they consistent, coherent, free of self-contradiction, do they adhere to the standards of intellectual credibility consistent with the kind of statements they are? For example, if we are making historical claims, we must use appropriate standards of historicity.

Women should not sell short this criterion of intellectual credibility, for the claims of a feminist theology, like the claims of any other Christian theology, must be able to be found intellectually credible even by those who do not hold its point of view. Feminists do make universal claims when they want others to see the validity of feminist points of view not just as one possible viewpoint but as one that must be taken seriously. Women, often stereotyped as irrational, should not foster this stereotype. This does not mean that purported standards of intellectual credibility cannot be examined and criticized by asking whether or not they serve the interests of particular groups of people. But it does mean that we should not pass over too quickly the search for such standards.

There is always the possibility that standards of credibility need to be revised and rethought, and this is what is happening

when one begins to see that credibility must be not only intellectual but also practical. For we must ask, second, are the
theological statements in question or their implications *practically* incredible? Do they serve the interests of one small segment
of the population against the interests of the whole? Notice here
that practical credibility extends not only to the words of any
theological formulation but beyond these words to the actions
or attitudes these statements or claims imply. So, although I have
claimed that theology is basically a verbal enterprise, one of
articulating rather than acting on the Christian faith, the implications of these verbal articulations for action have to be taken
very seriously indeed. Any theological claim or statement that
justifies male superiority or domination over women either explicitly or implicitly is practically incredible.

Judging a theology's credibility on the basis of its internal
coherence and noncontradiction alone leaves open the possibility that it can be used at best to condone the status quo and
at worst to sanction or even encourage continued oppression
on any number of bases. It is the lack of concern for the practical
dimension of credibility that has led to charges that theology is
separated from and sets itself above life, untouched by it but
still exercising enormous influence over it. It is the absence of
input from the experiences of non-persons that has prevented
white, male, middle-class, First-World theology from seeing its
limitations; what is practically incredible to others seems per-
fectly credible to many such theologians and theological audi-
ences.

As described in chapter 1, I use the term "norm" to indicate
the criterion or criteria by which any given theological sources
or formulations are judged to be adequate or inadequate for
theology. When I speak of women's experience as a norm for
theology, I mean one of the norms of practical credibility. Wom-
en's experience can and should be used as one of the major
criteria judging whether or not theology serves to exalt one group

(men) at the expense of another (women) and is therefore practically incredible to women. If it is practically incredible to wom-
en, it fails the test of credibility. (Of course, one could comment
on theology's practical incredibility from the points of view of
other oppressed groups as well.)

Insofar as Christian theology makes universal claims, either
explicitly or implicitly, women's experience of any of the types
named at the beginning of this chapter is one criterion for judging
these claims. Valerie Saiving's ground-breaking essay on sin (a
position further developed by Judith Plaskow) questions claims
that the traditional doctrine of "man" really includes everybody.[14]
Such questioning includes two sorts of discoveries. First was
the discovery (so clear in the Saiving essay) that, even if "man"
were meant to be a generic term, the "men" who were included
in the traditional understanding of sin were, in fact, males. Second, a development later than the Saiving article, was the discovery that "man" in fact had never been meant in a generic
sense and that in many ways women really had not ever been
(even peripherally) included in theology.[15]

Women's experience is a norm for theology when it is used
to show how certain claims to universality in theology are really
only claims for half the human race because the experience of
women has never even been considered. In formulating theological claims on the basis of women's experience, feminist
theologians have learned to make universal claims more spar-
ingly and to be more willing to see the diversity of humanity
around them.

Although there is great diversity in human experience, I do
not think that we have to give up entirely on the general or
universal. First, there are standards of rationality such as coherence and noncontradiction to which one can appeal, and
any theology should adhere to these standards. Second, although
the experiences of women and men in terms of reflected experience are in many ways vastly different, I do think that there
are certain shared characteristics. The human being is a being

of faith, faith that life, despite its difficulties and setbacks, is good. We live on the assumption that being alive is worthwhile and meaningful, that life is better than death. Even despair is a sign of life's meaning because one despairs in the face of something that one expects to be meaningful. It is this experience of faith, of hope, that I would name "religious" and our interpretations of that experience are partial and flawed human attempts, already overlaid with expectations and biases. Christians speak of this experience as experience of God, others name it in other ways.

Women's feminist experience (in concert with the recognition of women's socialized experience) is used as a norm for or judge of any theology insofar as that theology tries to limit women's abilities and roles by caricaturing women or by stereotyping them or by setting forth plain falsehood about women as truth. Together women's feminist experience and women's bodily experience are drawn on to counteract male myths about women's insatiable sexuality and therefore women's predisposition to sin and to tempt man to sin. Women's bodily experience is a norm to counteract male discussions of their own unruly and uncontrollable sexuality, which has given rise to fear of the body and the desire to separate mind or spirit from body and put the mind in control. The experiences of menstruation, pregnancy, and childbirth along with analysis of women's traditional experience of being totally identified with their bodies and women's feminist experience of, on the one hand, being wary of that total identification and yet, on the other, not being willing to separate themselves totally from nature, provide a cluster of women's experiences to judge the dualisms of traditional theology. The dualisms I have in mind here separate and rank mind or spirit over body or flesh, human over nature, and man and God together over woman.[16]

Both women's present experience and women's historical experience provide women of flesh and blood, three-dimensional women as foils for the stereotyped one-dimensional figures often found in theological discourse, thereby judging the traditional image and finding it wanting. In traditional theology women often appear only as temptress or virgin, as types, not as real women. Women's historical experience is normative insofar as it judges as partial traditional presentations of "human" experience and adds whole new dimensions to that experience.

Women's feminist experience exposes a patriarchal theology for what it is, half a theology, and judges it accordingly. In light of the discussion of sources above, women's experience provides the material for making half a theology a whole theology. Every theology has a point of view, and feminist theologians, by their conscious use of women's experience, own up to the point of view expressed in feminist theology. This then gives them the opportunity to judge theologies that claim to have no particular point of view, that claim to be totally objective. Women's experience provides a shared authority, a communal criterion, not just an individualistic one, for judging Christian theology. This helps to guard against both individualism and elitism in theology.

All historical traditions are selectively used by those who draw on them. Women's feminist experience coupled with women's historical experience points to the selectivity in Christian theology and judges it to be unrepresentative. Women's feminist experience is used to judge whether or not any given theology, or any part thereof, any theological claim or formulation liberates or oppresses women. As I will elaborate in the next chapter, I do not think, however, that women's experience by itself can be the sole criterion used to judge elements as adequate to or useful for Christian theology.

By themselves, what I speak of as women's individual experiences cannot be normative, but they do add to the richness and depth of any Christian theology.

Women's Experience and
Schüssler Fiorenza, Ruether, Russell

It is on the question of women's experience that there is most agreement in feminist theology. It is our experience of patriarchy, our experience of ourselves and other women as oppressed, that provides the starting point of feminist theology in women's experience. With Schüssler Fiorenza, Ruether, and Russell, I see the sexism in the Christian tradition that makes necessary the call for change, the call to take seriously and foster in theology the full humanity of women. I with the three of them partake in the feminist consensus outlined in chapter 1.

As will no doubt be clear from the above discussion of sources for theology, I think Ruether's move to look to nontraditional sources for Christian theology an important and timely one. Whether we agree about how these sources might be normative will have to wait until the next chapter.

Russell's concerns and mine coincide when she says that one needs to draw on scientific knowledge as well as human experience, making a criterion like what I speak of as "intellectual credibility" necessary. Her notion that women contribute to the unfinished dimension of theology is very much in line with the view espoused in this book that women do not necessarily formulate theologies entirely different from those of men, but that they do have something to add to theology that we will not be fully able to appreciate or evaluate until it is added. Although I do agree with Ruether that women as subjects should be the center of feminist theology, insofar as a feminist theology begins and ends with women's experience in mind, I see this as a strategic move striving to bring women and their point of view into theology at all, a move in Christian theology that needs to take seriously the full personhood and salvific possibilities for all human beings.

While Russell thinks that the purpose of theology *is* action, I think of action as central to the living out of Christian faith, but being fostered by, being critically reflected on and evaluated by theology rather than being theology's own purpose.

Russell's call for partnership, shared authority, and Schüssler Fiorenza's and Ruether's appeals to women-church seem to me much the same as the appeal here to the shared authority that arises when one uses women's experience and not any single individual's experience as a norm in Christian theology. The appeal is to the collectivity of women as a source of authority rather than to one individual or group of individuals set above all others.

It is, however, when Schüssler Fiorenza begins to speak of feminist theology as accountable only to women in the churches or when Ruether speaks of "practical eclecticism" that I begin to think about the question of how feminists who want also to do Christian theology are bound to the Christian tradition. There is much more divergence in feminist theology when one begins to pursue this question, and this is the subject matter of the next chapter.

4/
THE PLACE OF CHRISTIAN TRADITION IN A CHRISTIAN FEMINIST THEOLOGY

In this chapter I will turn to the questions of why and how Christian tradition functions as source and norm for Christian feminist theology. I use the term "Christian tradition" very broadly to indicate the sum total of the Christian past and present. I use this term descriptively, not prescriptively, to talk about both the glorious and the ignominious, what we want to remember and what we would sooner forget.

In using "Christian tradition" descriptively, I do not make a distinction between Scripture and tradition but count both under the one heading, for Scripture is, after all, part of the tradition. Under this descriptive heading as well, I do not want yet to separate what has been central to the Christian movement from what has been on its fringes; I want to include not only what happened in church councils, but also in the church at prayer; not only the church of men, but also the church of women.

Christian Tradition as Source

All the feminists writing from within the Christian church draw on Christian tradition (in the broad sense defined above) as source for their theologies, source here understood as that which provides themes and clues, catalysts for theological thought. Recall, for example, from chapter 2 that Ruether lists among the sources of her theology Scripture, marginal and heretical Christian traditions, and the dominant tradition in Christian theology. Likewise, Schüssler Fiorenza sees Scripture in particular and a more broadly defined Christian tradition in general as important sources in her theological thinking. What she calls the "Jesus movement," the inclusive movement that gathered around Jesus and was influenced by his teachings, is important for her as one place where women were truly accepted and welcomed. Russell emphasizes the importance of the whole of Christian tradition as the place from which one distills or discerns the Tradition, *the dynamic relation of God with us* in handing over Jesus Christ into the hands of all generations and nations."[1] All three draw heavily for source material on the experiences of women *as Christians*, women over the centuries within or on the fringes of Christianity who have lived their lives in relationship to that tradition.

If "source" for theology means that which can act as stimulus for theological thought, that which provides themes and clues, then the whole of Christian tradition as defined above could be possible source material for theology. Here I think feminist theologians such as Ruether do a service to Christian theology in general by reminding us to look again at what in the tradition has been found marginal or heretical and to ask how we would evaluate such material today. Elaine Pagels, for instance, has asserted that one of the reasons many of the gnostic texts were branded heretical in the early church was that they gave a prominent place to women.[2] We need to keep such a possibility in mind as we reevaluate our Christian past. Historians of Christianity such as Eleanor McLaughlin also do Christian theology an important service when they uncover the lives of women in the church of the past, not women who were counted famous because they did what men did, but ordinary women, whose lives and writings (if they can be recovered) give us insight into the faith of the people at a given time.[3]

We should not forget that source material can act as negative example as well as positive. Any theologian draws on Christian tradition selectively. When using the source material of Christian tradition we always have to note what is selected, how and by whom things are put, and whose interests they serve. We cannot be blind to the political wrangling that went on in making theological decisions, decisions that are often taught to students of church history as though only one outcome were possible.

Christian Tradition as Norm

It is when we come to the question of why and how Christian tradition might function normatively for feminist theology that we find major disagreement among feminist theologians. Since there are two distinct questions involved here, I will deal with each separately. First, *why* should the Christian tradition or some part thereof be normative for Christian feminist theology? Second, in what way should the Christian tradition or a part thereof function normatively for a Christian feminist theology?

In chapter 3, I asserted that Christian theology deals with two central "givens," the received Christian witness and the situation today. I also asserted that any Christian theology must attempt to articulate the *Christian* faith as it understands that term. When I refer to a norm or norms drawn from the received Christian witness and used to judge whether or not a theological statement or claim could be said to be Christian, I will speak of it as the norm of appropriateness.[4] This criterion determines whether or not a given theological statement or formulation is *appropriate* to the Christian witness of faith, *appropriately* Christian.

I think that one of the main tendencies in Christian feminist theology today is what seems to be a move toward collapsing the criterion of appropriateness into the criterion of credibility, to speak as if all that is credible to the feminist is thereby *de facto* Christian. Schüssler Fiorenza seems to make this move, as does Ruether in her more recent writings. For these two and for many other feminist theologians, the adjective "Christian" in the term "Christian feminist theology" means that the feminist theologian sees herself as Christian, that the Christian church is where she finds her religious roots. At this point it is important to recall that Schüssler Fiorenza, for instance, specifically denies that there is anything from within the Christian tradition itself that is normative for Christian feminist theology. For her the only admissible norm is whether or not a given theology or its constitutive parts oppresses or liberates women. What liberates women is Christian.

But there are problems with this point of view. If the term "Christian" is used in the way Schüssler Fiorenza and others use it, it can only be used self-descriptively. If I see myself as part of the Christian tradition, I call myself Christian. Basically the person employing the term can use it however he or she wishes. This means, then, that whereas feminist theologians may claim the use of "Christian" for whatever liberates women, if there is nothing that can be derived from the tradition itself that can be used normatively to argue that this is what Christianity is all about, then others can use the tradition in less liberating ways.

For example, white South Africans who support apartheid might want to argue that what the term "Christian" means to them is anything that allows them to remain in their state of supremacy and domination over blacks. Now, while I find this as repugnant as other feminist theologians do, unless some norm can be derived from the tradition that allows us to say what is and what is not Christian, one could not argue against their claim.

If nothing can be seen as inherently liberating within the Christian tradition, one also wonders why those feminists who maintain such a position do not begin to look for or to claim as central other more unambiguously liberating texts and traditions and leave the biblical texts and tradition entirely. Of course, there is the matter of historical connection. One uses the tradition with which one is connected by birth or circumstance. But this alone would not be enough to keep me as a feminist within the Christian church if I really thought there was nothing inherently liberating to claim as my inheritance in the tradition. Moreover, there are many things in the tradition that one might not want to claim, even though one is connected to them through Christian history (the Inquisition and some of the more sordid aspects of the Crusades, for example). In addition, one is historically connected to other events and movements in the past at the same time that one is connected by birth or circumstance to Christian history. Why then should one employ the adjective "Christian," unless it means something more than mere circumstantial connection?

One of the fears that seems to motivate the desire to collapse the norm of appropriateness into the norm of credibility is the fear of the tyranny of the past, a fear that Christians in the present (in particular feminist Christians) will be in bondage to outmoded and patriarchal thought forms, a fear that Scripture and/ or tradition will be used to justify the status quo insofar as the position of women is concerned.

Indeed, much in Scripture and tradition is patriarchal. We have to be open to the possibility that it is wholly and unrelentingly patriarchal. And if it is wholly and unrelentingly patriarchal, why would a feminist still want to see herself within this tradition? One danger of ignoring the normativeness of the Christian tradition for Christian theology is that we might continue to remain in an irreformable tradition. The greater danger of ignoring the normativeness of Christian tradition is that we lose sight of what might be said to constitute the Christian tradition *as Christian*. We need, of course, to take the contemporary situation into consideration. If the core of any religious tradition is its capacity to meet the needs of its adherents, the needs of present adherents must be met or the religion loses its relevance.

But if that same religious tradition is to maintain any of its identity as a tradition, its theology must be in touch with what makes that particular religious tradition unique.

Every religious tradition has elements of both the universal and the particular. Feminists recognize the need for particularity when they emphasize the need for theology to deal with questions raised by women's experience. The varied aspects of women's experience, in turn, compel feminist theology to take account of particularity. Yet sometimes feminists ignore the particularity necessary to differentiate Christianity from Judaism, Islam, or "feminist humanism" (if I may coin such a term). If the differentiation is no longer important, feminist theologians should cease using the term "Christian."

It is not necessary to choose one criterion *or* the other—tradition or present experience, appropriateness or credibility—for the two criteria work together. The criterion of appropriateness allows us to answer the question, Is it Christian? The criterion of credibility allows us to answer the question, Is it both intellectually and practically credible?

Using the tradition alone as source does not make one a Christian. Ruether, for example, wants to use sources outside Christianity yet still see herself as a Christian. If I am correct in saying that virtually anything might constitute source or catalyst for Christian theology, then using Scripture or other parts of the tradition as source does not necessarily make something "Christian," for elements of many other traditions might also be source material for Christian theology.

What can be said to constitute the Christian tradition as Christian? Peter Slater, in *The Dynamics of Religion*, offers some useful thoughts on what defines any particular religious tradition. Slater speaks of a religious tradition as constituted by a group of primary symbols clustered around one central symbol. The content and emphasis of the primary symbols change over time, but the central symbol remains the same. It is the interaction between primary symbols and central symbol that determines how a religious tradition is seen in any given time and place.

For Slater, primary symbols are "central to the development of a particular religious tradition,"[5] but they are not symbols that cannot be given up or modified. The primary symbols help impart to a tradition its distinctive character. Feminist theologians have discovered that a primary symbol like that of the fatherhood of God must be either given up or its usage broadened to include as primary other symbols as well. Thus, one hopes, as primary symbols are given up or modified according to feminist critique, the "distinctive character" of patriarchy in Christianity will also be given up or modified. The central symbol of a tradition is, for Slater, the symbol that "consistently holds *the* central position."[6]

> A central symbol is that in a tradition which enables its exponents to organize their perceptions and express their vision of their way in life toward the realization of some transcendent end. . . . The central symbol provides the nucleus around which other symbols are clustered to develop a particular pattern of faith. . . . The interactions between this symbol and the changing roster of primary and secondary symbols are what define the meaning of being Christian or Buddhist or whatever at a given moment in history.[7]

Slater speaks of changing the primary symbols as "a reformation" and changing the central symbol as "radical conversion."[8] His accounting of primary symbols and central symbol allows for historical development and change within a given tradition, but it also allows some way besides self-description alone for that tradition to be identified. If one appeals only to a member's self-identification as a criterion for deciding what is or is not part of a given religious tradition, one is left with a relativism that must accept all without judgment or discernment.

Such a descriptive criterion may be useful for the historian who is trying to understand the pluriformity of what has called itself Christian, but it is of limited usefulness to the theologian who is trying to articulate a fully reflective and fully critical understanding of Christianity rather than accepting all its forms and formulations *a priori* as of equal validity and weight. Although traditions often have a certain fluidity of relationship to one another, they nonetheless have their own unique and specific identities, products of the historical context in which they arose and developed and the symbols that set them apart in their development from other traditions with which they interact. If the notion of being an adherent of one religious tradition and not another is to have any rational content, it must be derived in part from the symbols that give that tradition an identity through time.

For Slater, Jesus the Christ is the central symbol in Christianity. The interpretation of the symbol is variable, allowing for growth or diversity of understanding. But the symbol remains central. When it ceases to be central, the religious tradition in question ceases to be Christianity.

Slater's view rings true in Christian experience. Christianity as a religion arose around the event of Jesus' life and death. Christians are the people who make the central claim that Jesus is the Christ, or Lord, or Savior, or any one of a number of other titles that are ascribed to him. To make this claim is not, of course, to say *prima facie* that there are no other Christs, but what it does say is that if one does not claim Jesus as the Christ *in some way*, one is not dealing with Christianity but with something different, something with a different central symbol. Perhaps in the same way that Christianity ceased to be part of Judaism when it was seen to have a central symbol different from Torah—the central symbol of Judaism—(even though some primary symbols remained shared), some feminisms that have their genesis in Christianity have ceased to share its central symbol.

Feminists are not the only ones to have moved away from Jesus as the Christ as central symbol. Others have done the same in the name of genuine pluralism. Tom Driver, for instance, in *Christ in a Changing World* advocates that we not place Jesus Christ at the center of all things, for he thinks that such a focus has kept us fixed on the past in such a way that we are not open to God's action in the present.[9] The focus on the past he thinks also causes a Christocentrism that has kept Christians closed to seeing God's work in other religious traditions.

Driver thinks that Christians must cease to focus on "Christ past" and focus instead on a Christ who is to come.[10] But this is, I submit, to change the central symbol from Jesus the Christ to some other Christ. It is also to ignore the fact that one can embrace a religious tradition in all its particularity without making exclusive claims for it, without implying that the truth expressed within it is expressed only there and nowhere else. Particularity and exclusivity do not need to go hand in hand.

In her earlier work Rosemary Radford Ruether appealed to what she called the "prophetic-liberating" or "prophetic-messianic" tradition as normative, that tradition, derived from the prophets of the Hebrew Bible and above all from Jesus, which supports and encourages the overcoming of oppression.[11] But in her more recent work, Ruether has moved away from the notion of this prophetic-liberating tradition as normative, seeing it instead as only one source of a theology whose norm is women's experience of liberation. She does this in the name of "feminist ecumenism," but, as I said above in relation to Driver, surely ecumenism does not always mean abandoning everything that differentiates one's tradition from another.

I am not saying that every legitimate theology is a Christian theology. There can be many useful and valuable and credible theologies that are not Christian theologies. The point to be made here is that if theologies claim to be Christian they must seek to be clear about the force of that adjective in relation to the theology.

I have made a claim that the central symbol in Christianity is Jesus as the Christ, but that does not answer one very important question, the question of how this symbol relates to whatever might be said to be normative in Christian tradition.

How does one get from the central symbol of Jesus Christ to some norm for Christian theology? How should the Christian tradition or some part thereof function as norm for Christian feminist theology? Such questions will form the starting point for the next section of this chapter.

How Should Christian Tradition Be Normative?

If one agrees that for the adjective "Christian" to mean anything in Christian feminist theology one must somehow see the Christian tradition as normative over that theology, one is still left with the enormous task of deciding just what within the tradition is normative and how one should appeal to that normative element or elements in one's theology.

To appeal to the whole of Christian tradition (Scripture included) is to appeal to something both contradictory and unwieldy. What has been considered within the pale of Christendom over its two millennia of existence has varied, and to appeal to the whole of Christian tradition is to beg the question, since one has to sort out that tradition and make some priorities among its multifariousness before one can appeal to it as norm.

One way to organize the tradition is to allow or to accept a voice of authority, the magisterium, as determiner of the norm. The *New Catholic Encyclopedia* defines the magisterium as the "perennial, authentic and infallible teaching office committed to the apostles by Christ and now possessed and exercised by their legitimate successors, the college of bishops in union with the pope."[12] In this traditional Roman Catholic understanding, the magisterium of pope and bishops is the final authority in determining what is normatively Christian. But even the magisterium, ground of final appeal that it is in the Roman Catholic

Church, does not function independently of Scripture and tradition but is supposed to allow itself to be normed by that Scripture and tradition.[13]

I see the move by Schüssler Fiorenza and other feminist theologians to establish women's experience as the court of last appeal in Christian theology as an attempt to develop an alternative magisterium.[14] One can hardly blame them for a healthy feminist skepticism about and rejection of a norm that by definition excludes women from among the decision makers. Why should women, who have been wronged and oppressed by the church, follow the teachings of a magisterium that shows no indication of wanting to include them as full and valuable human beings?

I do not think it incidental that most of the women who appeal to an alternative magisterium have their roots in Roman Catholic Christianity, for what they are seeking to do is to substitute a magisterium that includes women's experience for one that excludes it. They have traded an oppressive magisterium for one that has the possibility of offering liberation. But in so doing, these feminist theologians have self-consciously adopted a stance that, to my mind, embraces one of the biggest problems in the exercise of the traditional Roman Catholic magisterium before it. This stance is the refusal to let oneself be normed by anything within the tradition itself. One of the criticisms that could be levied at certain points in Roman Catholic doctrinal history is that the magisterium lost sight of the tradition it was serving and made its doctrinal decisions *sui generis*. This is, it seems to me, exactly what is happening when women's experience is made the only norm for judging Christian theology. It is true in the case of feminist theology that by such a criterion theology ceases to be oppressive, and that is all to the good. The danger, however, is that it ceases also to be anything that could rightly be called "Christian."

It is perhaps a Protestant predisposition here, but what I cannot support in a magisterium of pope and bishops, I cannot support in a magisterium of women's experience alone either. Again, I want to make it clear that the criterion of women's experience is all-important to a feminist theology. But women's experience as the only criterion of judgment is necessary *but not sufficient* as the norm for a Christian feminist theology.

To speak of Protestant predisposition here is, no doubt, to raise the issue of the traditional Protestant criterion *sola scriptura*. Appealing to Scripture is a little less unwieldy than appealing to all of Scripture and tradition, but there are several points to consider. First, Scripture *is* tradition, tradition that has historically been given a place of prominence in the church, but tradition nonetheless. We know that the writings we have as the Bible are creations of many different authors. We know that the Gospels, in particular, are compilations of materials from various sources. We know that other similar materials exist that are not part of the New Testament. There is no firm dividing line between Scripture and tradition, and therefore there is nothing inherent that would mark Scripture as a whole as norm over and against tradition.

Second, Scripture, even the New Testament, being composed of a variety of sources, expresses not one point of view but many. Are all these expressions equally normative? Since feminist questions have impelled us here, let me use as an example certain texts about women. First Corinthians 14 says women should keep silent in the churches; 1 Corinthians 11 assumes that women are praying and prophesying, and asks only that they cover their heads when they do so; in the Gospels women are sent to proclaim the good news. How can these and many other examples that could have been offered be sorted out?

I would suggest that we can sort this out following in spirit if not in letter the same norm that Martin Luther used. Although the Reformers are associated with the term *sola scriptura*, Luther did not, in fact, appeal to all of Scripture as uniformly useful and usable. It is well known that he thought the Epistle of James was an "epistle of straw" and he wondered how it had ever gotten into the New Testament canon.

Luther thought that one judged the "Christian-ness" of Scripture and tradition according to whether or not it set forth Jesus Christ. And here, although Luther and I might disagree in the end about specific details, separated as we are by the advent of historical criticism, I think that Luther was profoundly right. Scripture, tradition, magisterium—none of these three exists on its own, independently of Jesus who has come to be called the Christ. It is around him and because of him that Christianity exists at all. And here we return to the argument above that Jesus Christ is the central symbol of Christianity.

If Jesus is the central symbol of Christianity, surely the norm for judging whether something is or is not Christian is derived from Jesus. But how do we move from symbol to norm? One popular way to derive such a norm is to attempt to make the historical Jesus himself that norm, to use the best of historical criticism to sort out what Jesus said and did from later traditions about him. But Jesus is not directly accessible to us. He did not write a book, and the reports we have of him are filtered through the witness of others, the witness of those who were so moved by him that they told the stories they knew about him to others; the witness of those who, somewhere along the line, wrote those stories down; the witness of those we know as Matthew, Mark, Luke, and John, who compiled the Gospels as we have them.

Because of the way these stories come to us, because we know that they are cast with the imprints of their authors and editors, because they are not biographical data but witness of faith, because we have no other independent access to Jesus, we can never know absolutely just what Jesus said and did. The writers and redactors of the Gospels want not so much to write biographies as they want to witness to their faith in this person, and they want to bring us to that same faith.

Historically we do not have access to Jesus; we have access to earlier and later witness about him. On the surface, we might be sorry about this. It would be so much better, we might think, if Jesus had written something directly himself. Then we would know what was really normative. But would we? Unless I know not only about Jesus but also about the effect he had on his followers, I have not understood his importance. The world was full of miracle workers and teachers. Why is it this one in whom I am called to have faith? Because some came to faith through him and wanted others to know it. The faith of the earliest followers that this Jesus was special, significant, sent by God, is the human response to this divine event. Both the bare event of Jesus and human response to it are necessary for Christianity to be.

Historically we cannot get back to the bare event of Jesus; theologically we do not need to. This does not mean, however, that we do not need the help of historical criticism to determine what are the earliest strands of the tradition in the Gospels. We need the results of historical criticism so that we will be able to get back as close as possible to the witness of the earliest apostles, for to understand the faith to which they felt themselves called is to come to an understanding of the faith to which we also are called. We come to faith in Jesus with the apostles, but it is also *through* their faith that we come to faith. Their witness of faith teaches us what this faith in Jesus Christ is. It teaches us who Jesus was for them and therefore who he can and should be for us. We look to the witness of faith of the earliest layer of tradition because it constitutes the later Christian tradition, formative and informative for all that comes after it.

In *The Point of Christology*, Schubert M. Ogden argues that although we should still appeal with the Reformers to apostolicity as a criterion for canonicity, a new understanding of what constitutes apostolicity and therefore the normative canon for theology is in order. We now know that what the Reformers took to be the criterion setting Scripture apart from tradition, that is, apostolic authorship, cannot be, strictly speaking, asserted of any of the New Testament sources. But apostolicity can be located elsewhere. The apostolic witness is not the whole of the New Testament but the earliest layer of witness one can discern within it. This becomes, for Ogden, the new norm of appropriateness, the canon *before* the canon. Ogden sees this earliest stratum of witness, the witness of the apostles, as authority authorized by Jesus, the "primal source" of this authority. In this regard Ogden also argues that whatever access one has to Jesus one cannot see him as just an authority; one must see him as the primal *source* of authority.

> It lies in the very logic of the concept of "authority" that the primal *source* of authority, whether implicit or explicit, cannot itself be *an* authority, at least in the same literal sense of the word. On the other hand, and by the same logic, there belongs to the original authority authorized by its primal source, and so in this case to the witness of the apostles as explicitly authorized by Jesus, the unique role of also being the originating authority and therefore the sole primary norm or canon. This is so because it is solely through this original and originating authority that the primal source authorizing it is explicitly available precisely as such.[15]

Jesus is available to us only through the witness of the apostles. Through historical criticism we discover the earliest witness to him. He is not the norm of appropriateness, but as central symbol of Christianity he is the source of that norm, in Ogden's words the "primary authorizing source." The norm of appropriateness, authorized by Jesus, is the earliest stratum of tradition that one can ascertain by historical criticism. In this layer we come to understand who Jesus was for the earliest apostles and who he can and should be for us.

If, formally, the norm for appropriateness is the earliest stratum of witness in the New Testament, what does this mean in material terms? Even though I do not believe that one can reach the historical Jesus by discerning the earliest layer of the tradition, I do believe that one can uncover what constitutes earlier and later parts of the tradition. First, New Testament scholars generally agree that the earliest layer of the tradition is to be found in the Synoptic Gospels. Second, most historical critics agree that the kingdom or reign of God was central to Jesus' message in this earliest layer of tradition although it is a matter of some dispute exactly how the kingdom is to be understood.[16] In light of the reign of God pressing in upon the world, Jesus called his followers to repent, to believe his message. As Herbert Braun says, "Jesus did not intend to *give information* about the imminent end, but to *summon* people because of it."[17] Braun does not see the importance of Jesus' message to lie in rules and regulations but in its call to love God and neighbor. For Braun, love of God was reinterpreted by Jesus in terms of love of one's neighbor. One could only love God through loving the neighbor.

Willi Marxsen says:

> It is characteristic of the Jesus kerygma [Marxsen's term for the earliest layer of tradition] that apocalyptic details are sharply reduced. It is really only the framework that remains, and questions about the coming state of affairs are rejected; it will be entirely different from the way anyone can imagine here on earth (Mark 12:25). Moreover, Jesus was not understood as an apocalyptic teacher who (like many before and after him and like the sect of Qumran in his own time) supposed that there was still a period of time before the coming of the kingdom, even though a very brief one. Jesus' hearers understood him to mean that there was no more time.[18]

Neither Braun nor Marxsen thinks that Jesus asked his hearers to affirm him as messiah.[19] The attribution of such titles came later as the followers tried to make sense of who this person was through whom they had come to new understandings of God and themselves. Jesus did call them to faith *in* God *through* himself.[20] And the God in whom they were called to have faith was a God of benevolent providence, a personal God.[21] Jesus demanded decision from his followers, decision about God, about himself, about the neighbor. According to Pheme Perkins, "The presumption is that the disciple is whole-heartedly pursuing righteousness even at considerable personal cost and suffering."[22] Through Jesus, his hearers knew the presence of God in their midst. As Dibelius says, Jesus signaled threat, promise and demand to those who heard him.[23] Marxsen confirms this: "In the 'repetition' of the preaching of Jesus and in the presentation of his activity, those who have encountered him give expression to their experiences with Jesus. In so doing they present him as the one who has appeared to them, the one who has prompted and initiated these experiences in them."[24]

Jesus is not the one who sets rules but the one who summons his hearers to respond to the imminent reign of God, to respond to the grace of God, to respond to the demand of God placed before us in the neighbor; a summons, a grace, a demand that they have come to know *through him.* If we look for specific rules for conduct in specific cases we will be disappointed. The texts do not contain this sort of evidence, and, further, what we know from the earliest layers of the tradition suggests that looking for such rules is inappropriate.[25] The call to love God and neighbor is always a call to discern what in each case is the loving thing. The normative character of this earliest witness lies not in specifics (What exact words did he say? What precisely did he do?) but in the experience of God's love and the call to love both God and neighbor in response that he represents. Jesus is, in this earliest layer of tradition, not primarily *exemplum*, example, but primarily *sacramentum*, sacrament, making God present in the midst of the people, because it was specifically through him and not some other that people felt themselves addressed by God. As sacrament, Jesus *is* the presence of God and not just a symbol of this presence or a pointer to it. The message of the Gospels does not bind us to particular acts but to a particular attitude. The apostolic witness records the response of believers as a response not to God in the abstract but to God through Jesus.

Working from a different angle, what he calls the "criterion of adequacy" (i.e., "that is original which best explains the multiplicity engendered in the tradition"), John Dominic Crossan's understanding of Jesus is remarkably similar in its conclusions to the general outline presented here.[26] *"First, the message of Jesus was a proclamation of the unmediated presence of God. . . . Second, this permanent availability of God knew no limits of time or space, doctrine or practice, text or book, power or wealth, family, rank or status. . . . Third, this immediacy of God to humans involves a reciprocal immediacy of humans to one another. . . . Fourth, this proclamation was radically simple, profoundly paradoxical, and politically explosive."*[27]

To center on a norm derived from the biblical witness is a move I share with Rosemary Ruether in her early work and with Letty Russell. Ruether in her early work appeals to the "prophetic-liberating" tradition derived from the Bible as normative. She sees this prophetic-liberating tradition displayed thematically throughout the Bible, in the Hebrew scriptures and in the New Testament, particularly in the prophets and in Jesus. No doubt the theme to which she points is a major one in the Bible, although there is always disagreement about what constitute the Bible's central themes. The implications of her choice are certainly consistent with the implications of the earliest layer of tradition in the Synoptic Gospels. But we differ in three regards.

First, I would say that the choice of the prophetic-liberating theme as central to Christianity must itself be authorized by something beyond itself, more central to the Christian tradition than the theme itself, that it must be authorized by Jesus whom Christians call the Christ. And this points to the second area of difference. Ruether has always strongly maintained that Jesus points beyond himself to a messiah to come and that for Christians to see him with finality even for themselves is exclusionary and anti-Semitic. As is clear from the above arguments, I think Jesus is central to Christianity. I do not think that this is necessarily and inevitably a mark of anti-Semitism, but only a mark of the particularity of religious traditions. To call him the Messiah as Christians came to do does not necessarily mean that there are no other messiahs, nor does it mean that everyone else must accept him as such at their peril. Christians are the people who call Jesus the Christ, the Savior, the Lord.

A third area of difference separates my position from Russell's position and Ruether's. When both Ruether and Russell appeal to Jesus, they appeal to him first of all as example. Now, while the record of the Gospels about him undoubtedly portrays him as a good example to follow, especially where women are concerned, and while I am happy to appeal to his example as useful and helpful in many cases, I do not see his function primarily as example but as the sacrament of the presence of God in the midst of humanity, issuing a call to response. The danger of seeing Jesus primarily as example is that it might be used to restrict conduct to Jesus' specific action at a specific time. The examples we have are limited; we cannot be positive of the historicity of all that we have and much that Jesus said and did we do not have. Take the instance of Jesus' teachings on divorce. If we take Jesus primarily as example, we might say, "See, he prohibits divorce except for adultery. We should do likewise." And this would, at one level, be true if we concentrate on the example alone without extrapolating beyond it to understand the point of Jesus' life and the much broader function he plays in the lives of Christians. Also, by concentrating on example, we run a much greater risk of allowing first-century patriarchal biases to determine Christian teaching. To use Jesus primarily as example often does not take account of the earlier and later layers of the Gospels either, thus esteeming all stories and sayings of Jesus equally valuable.

Russell and I agree that the center of Christianity is Jesus the Christ, although as mentioned above, she appeals to him as example. But another major difference between her position and mine is that she places emphasis on the utopian future, and I place emphasis on the present. She sees the Word of God as oriented to the future, calling us toward the future, and I see the gospel message as pointing to the necessity of present action. It is not some utopian future beckoning us forward that impels us, but God's demand for action in the present. We both want the same things, but we see the emphasis differently.

Why Such a Norm Can Be Useful for Feminists

The biggest fear that feminist theologians have in tying themselves to some norm derived from the Christian tradition is that they will be linked inextricably with a patriarchal tradition. In the earliest layer of tradition no mention is made of male or female. No distinction is made between men and women. All are offered God's salvation and called to decision about God's love. What this means, then, is that when one raises the question of credibility to women in the context of the norm of appropriateness, one discovers that what is normative from Christian tradition is not practically incredible to women. But patriarchal notions have certainly encroached on this earliest layer of tradition. Admittedly, one is called to that decision by a male savior figure (and the significant question of the importance of his maleness will be raised in the next chapter), but if I am correct, one cannot move away from this central figure and still remain within the Christian tradition. The one who calls, however, extends that call to all, women as well as men.

The norm to which I appeal is, as it turns out, not one that feminists need to fear. The call of Jesus is not tied to first-century conditions, it allows for a response in one's own time and place. It is a call that, first, shows forth God's love. It is also a call to respond to the love of God in one's own life, but not in a life in isolation, for the call of God is extended to all and the love of God encompasses all God's creatures. It is not a call to the isolated individual to be saved, to worry only about his or her personal relationship with God. It is a call to individuals, to be sure, but to individuals inextricably connected with other individuals, both human and nonhuman in the world around them.

If the love of God is all-encompassing, if it does not respect the boundaries we as humans have drawn between one another and between ourselves and the rest of God's creation, then the call to respond does not let us love only those we want to love. When we are called to respond to God, we are called to love those whom God loves and to love them as God loves, insofar as that is humanly possible.

To love all whom God loves is to desire the best for each one, its own best, the best it is capable of and can aspire to. In these days when we know that our societal structures are not divinely dictated but humanly created, we can see how often these structures get in the way of human individuals aspiring to their best, or of nonhuman creatures living to their own capacities. We can see the need for the social structures that enslave us to be replaced by social structures that free us from oppression. The demand of the gospel in the twentieth century is not just that we be moral as individuals; it is a demand to change immoral social structures. The message of the gospel is a message of liberation. What it says for women is that the love of God desires women to exercise their full potential as whole human beings. In the twentieth century this means recognizing the structures that have kept women from doing this.

It is here that we come full circle to the norm of credibility, for it is the incredibility of so many of these structures in our day that sets us on this search in the first place. And here the norms of credibility and appropriateness come together. It might not have been so. Conceivably we could have discovered that the tradition was, at its root, irreformably patriarchal. If so, feminists should abandon it, and a feminist Christian theology would not be possible. But I am convinced that what is central to the tradition, despite Christianity's mottled past, is not inherently patriarchal, although in much of its history it has been lived and taught in a patriarchal way.

Some feminists may see my position as hopelessly naïve. How can I believe that a tradition so steeped in patriarchy could change? Am I making a desperate attempt to rescue that which defies rescue? I have not intended here to exonerate Christian history, nor have I intended to deny the intertwining of Christian history and patriarchy in what to some seems an inextricable fashion. Nor, as I hope I have made clear, do I think that Christian theology is the only legitimate and useful theology.

What I have been trying to do, though, is first to see what is central to Christianity and second to see if what is central is or is not patriarchal. No matter how many feminists opt out of Christianity (and I know there are many good reasons for making that decision) there will still be those who call themselves Christian. One reason to keep trying to do a feminist Christian theology is for all those women (many of whose lives might still be untouched by feminism, but whose lives are deeply influenced by patriarchy) who for whatever reasons are still within the Christian church. To attempt a Christian feminist theology is to refuse to give up on those women; it is also to refuse to leave one whole segment of the world's population given over to patriarchy without a struggle. The theology presented here is one way to keep up that struggle.

How do the two norms relate to one another? I suggest that neither takes precedence. A theological statement that claims to be Christian but is not credible is no more valid for a Christian theology than one that is credible but bears no explicit relation to the Christian witness of faith. The norms are always applied together, they are not at war with each other. It is not a relationship of adversaries but one of complementary principles. It is only when they are taken as adversaries that arguments over which takes precedence arise.

Much of what has been said here has shown the norms of appropriateness and crediblity in criticism of existing theologies.

What remains is to put these principles into practice, to test them, to show how they would work in actually formulating a Christian feminist theology. This is what the next chapter will do briefly for two theological topics, christology and ecclesiology.

5/
THE METHOD ENACTED: CHRIST AND CHURCH

In this final chapter I want to put into practice the method I have espoused. I do this by outlining briefly how the method might be applied to the theological themes of christology and ecclesiology, two of the many themes in traditional theology that are of concern to feminists.

The norms of appropriateness and credibility provide a framework, a structure for Christian theology. They provide boundaries beyond which, at least according to this writer, an adequate Christian theology cannot transgress. That said, however, the possibilities within those boundaries are still wide open. A theology can be formulated in many different ways, and this is where the matter of source material becomes paramount. For once the outlines are drawn, the theologian fills them in with material drawn from a variety of sources.

Here I will provide no more than a structure and a few suggestions or clues to begin filling in the structure. When I deal with christology I will concentrate particularly on the question of how Jesus' maleness is or is not an issue for a Christian feminist theology. With regard to ecclesiology, I am particularly interested in the issues of church structure and leadership.

Christology

The criterion of intellectual credibility tells us that we must not claim anything incoherent or contradictory for theology. One of the implications of this criterion for christology, I think, is that we cannot claim for the action of God in Jesus Christ anything that contravenes what we would claim as possible actions of God elsewhere. By this statement I mean that if one's christology implies an intervention of God directly in the events of the world, causing just this event and no other to happen in just this particular way, with particular and specific human responses to this event, then one also has to reckon with the possibility of direct interventions of God in every other place in history. Or, conversely, if one does not expect God to intervene to stop a truck from going over the edge of a cliff, to prevent a tumor from growing, or unilaterally to bring about world peace, if one does not expect God to contravene creaturely freedoms, then one has to ask whether and how far one's own christology is in line with these premises when one ponders other theological questions.

In line with the criterion of intellectual credibility, one must also raise questions about how far the Chalcedonian language of nature and person is credible or even intelligible for persons of today.

If I am correct in my claims in the last chapter, to deal with Christianity is to deal with *Jesus* as the Christ. But this raises a question that feminists cannot avoid, for Jesus was a male. And the question is, therefore, Can a feminist theology come to terms with his maleness? In what ways does his maleness create problems for a Christian feminist theology?

Some feminists would say that by my insistence on seeing Jesus as central to Christianity I have already made it impossible to be both feminist and a Christian, for what feminist would be satisfied to worship or to claim a male savior figure? Indeed, one of the central reasons Mary Daly moved out of Christianity was because she saw it as inseparably connected with a male God and a male savior, making maleness part of Christianity's essence, and she saw that as too much for a feminist to accept. I think, however, that one needs to look further before dismissing belief in Jesus as the Christ as incredible simply because of his maleness.

It is clear that a christology that emphasizes Jesus' maleness by claiming thereby that maleness is the normative form of humanity or that maleness is essential to his salvific role is practically incredible to women because it would serve to exalt maleness over femaleness and therefore males over females. It is just this that happens in the "Vatican Declaration: Women in the Ministerial Priesthood." One of the arguments against the ordination of women is that since the priest represents Christ to the people, and is Christ's "very image, when he pronounces the words of consecration" this priest must bear a "natural resemblance" to Christ in his maleness.[1] If the priest were not a man, one could not see in this priest the image of Christ. "For Christ was and remains a man."[2]

The document hastens to add that Christ abolishes the distinctions between Jew and Greek, slave and free, male and female. "Nevertheless, the incarnation of the word took place according to the male sex; this is indeed a question of fact, and this fact, while not implying an alleged natural superiority of man over woman cannot be disassociated from the economy of salvation; it is, indeed, in harmony with the entirety of God's plan as God himself has revealed it, and of which the mystery of the covenant is the nucleus."[3] God has chosen to send Christ, the bridegroom, to his bride, the church. Christ's maleness is of such central importance, according to this Vatican document, that it serves to exclude women from certain functions in the church.

Any christology that sees Jesus' maleness as indicative of the maleness of God is also incredible according to the criterion of women's experience, for it too would seem to give maleness an exalted position, more like God than femaleness is. Mary Daly's "if God is male, then the male is God" seems apropos here.[4] The maleness of God could be questioned on the grounds of intellectual credibility as well, for any God that could be either male or female could not be the kind of God whom Christians claim. Any God who is the universal, omnipresent God Christians claim is not subject to the biological definitions and limitations of human beings.

Some (the Vatican document, for example) have argued that God's choice to incarnate Godself in a male human being must be all-important. God chose a male and not a female. That must mean something. But my own understanding of God's action in the world (an understanding, I would claim, within the bounds of intellectual credibility) makes it difficult to claim a particular and specific choice on the part of God for a male savior to the exclusion of a female.

It is very difficult in the late twentieth century to think of God as intervening directly in history. As Bultmann pointed out, we live in a closed world.[5] We do not expect God to come sweeping in at any moment; indeed, we live on the premise that this will not happen. If we drop something we expect the force of gravity to pull it toward the floor, where the impact may break it. We expect certain effects from certain causes.

God as universal is always and everywhere related to the world. God does not coerce or control events, yet God underlies, is present, and responds to things that happen. To say that God underlies all that happens is to say that the boundaries of our world have been established by God, but within these boundaries we exercise our creaturely freedoms. If God does not coerce our actions or those of anything else in creation, then, through our exercise of freedom, all that happens is not necessarily good.

God's response to our action is to will us to make the best of each new situation, to work in each new moment for the best. Some people are unsatisfied with such a role for God, thinking that it disempowers God. But the alternative seems to me to be the model of the despot who exercises power arbitrarily, who without reason pardons some and condemns others to death.

In Christian terms, the relationship of human beings to God might be called grace or revelation. People are constantly in

God's presence, constantly recipients of God's revelation whether they are explicitly conscious of it or not. At times, this grace, this presence of God which is always and everywhere available, is "objectified" in historical events, that is, human beings encounter events in their history that they recognize as a fitting historical exemplification of the experience of God's grace that has continuously surrounded them.[6] Such an event must show forth God in God's love and care for the world but must also be recognized by persons as an event of revelation in order to be such.

Although for Christians it is in Jesus that they see God's presence, God's love and care exemplified, that this decisive revelation has taken place in a man, is, in a very real sense, accidental. There could be any number of historical events that could re-present God's grace to persons in a definitive way. From God's point of view, females are as apt as males to be such representative figures. God's grace, as universal, is not a respecter of persons. It is human social structures and not God's choice that make the appearance of a male savior figure more likely. God did not choose Jesus in the sense that God chose him above all others. Rather, God chose Jesus as God could choose many other events that are fitting re-presentations of God's grace. After God's choice must come human recognition for an event to be seen as God's action or revelation.

Although God's re-presentation of Godself to Christians takes a male form, this can in no way be used to argue that God could never be re-presented in a female form. However, because of our long history of the oppression and degradation of women, patriarchal cultures and societies are more apt to recognize the re-presentation of God in a male.[7] And so in reference to a male savior, the "choice" is more human than divine. The maleness of Jesus does not automatically exclude him from being able to re-present God's grace to women.

With regard to what the savior does, the work of salvation, given what women have learned through what I have called feminist experience about interpreting their bodily experience, no savior would be credible whose offer of salvation extended only to a disembodied soul. Salvation is credible to the feminist only if it includes the whole human being, rather than fragmenting or dichotomizing the human being, and, in turn, dichotomizing human beings into the more "bodily" ones and the more "spiritual" ones.

Salvation and a savior who offers it are also incredible to the feminist if some human beings as a group appear to be inherently more suitable candidates for salvation or more easily saved than others. In many places throughout the history of the church, women have been branded as the greater sinners and as those who sin further in that they tempt men to sin. A credible savior offers salvation to all human beings equally. He or she is not a respecter of persons.

Further, a salvation that is individual, personal, and private, that has no social implications is incredible to the feminist. Such a salvation could not possibly speak to the deepest needs of someone struggling to be liberated from the yoke of oppression. The only meaningful salvation for the feminist is one that has social consequences, where, whatever else might also be at stake, one of the results is the overcoming of the social structures that promote oppression. This also rules out as incredible any salvation that is totally otherworldly, directed to some world beyond this one, not to change in this world. Whatever they may think about the possibilities of a world to come, feminists want change in this world, the only world we have, know, and can deal with now. Feminists recognize that our social structures are not divinely ordained but humanly created and, as such, can be humanly changed if the will to change is truly there.

Along with other human beings, feminists are engaged in the search for meaning and purpose in their lives, for affirmation that the sense they have that life is meaningful, is justified. A credible savior would be one who can impart the reassurance needed and who can do this by offering the possibility of a

salvation that heals the whole self and the whole society, a
salvation that is this-worldly and inclusive.

Given that these are the concerns of credibility, what is
offered in the witness to Jesus in the earliest layer of the synoptic
tradition (the apostolic tradition as the norm of appropriateness
for which I have argued)? The apostolic tradition places no
particular emphasis on Jesus' maleness and none on the sex of
those called by him. There is no suggestion that some are more
easily saved than others, nor is there any suggestion that Jesus'
maleness has anything to do with his salvific purpose. Clearly
the stories of the calling of the Twelve are interlaced with (later)
symbolic purpose; their place as later tradition is also in evidence
in that the Gospels do not agree on the twelve names, only on
their number.

As I said in the previous chapter, the importance of Jesus
is as the one who calls others to respond to God through himself.
The emphasis is on Jesus as the one who re-presents God, who
presents again to the people the universal God of revelation. I
would say of this function of Jesus that it clearly connects him
as a human being to the divine. The divinity of Jesus is to be
understood by recognizing his function as a re-presentation of
God, not I would say, by trying to understand the unity of human
and divine as a combination of substances or natures.

But does this re-presentative function where a male is the
re-presentative imply the maleness of God? Clearly, if I am right
about how others, both male and female, might also be seen
as revealing God, as re-presentations of God, then the maleness
of one savior figure does not imply anything about the maleness
of God. Also, as I argued in the last section, as much as Christians
have implied the maleness of God by what they have said, such
maleness, given what Christians have understood by the concept
of "God," is incredible.

Even if, in the earliest tradition, Jesus called God "Father,"
this is not our only or even our primary option. Because I have
argued that it is primarily not as example that we appeal to Jesus

but as sacrament of God's presence, his practice is not necessarily always to be emulated with painstaking exactness as though his example (however historical) provides rules to be followed. I see no need to restrict the names for God to those which Jesus is said to have used. There are many scriptural names and images for God that are not placed on Jesus' lips, yet they are useful and evocative ways to address and speak of God.

In addition, what might the term "Father" be taken to imply? Surely it does not indicate maleness, or even male-likeness, but says God is the kind of God who enters into a particular kind of relationship, a relationship of love, of closeness, of caring and concern. We should not be surprised that the same first-century world that recognized Jesus as Messiah should hear from his lips the male language for God to which they were accustomed. Jesus shows us who God is, not as male, but as love.

What is the salvation Jesus offers? It is composed of two elements: the divine call through Jesus and the human response to that call. What Jesus offers to those who listen is God's love, God's grace, reassurance of human longings to be valuable, loved, cared for. God offers this love freely, to all, and here offers it through Jesus. But this offer of love before we do anything to deserve it is also a call to respond, a demand. Grace comes before the demand but also implies the demand. For salvation offered and salvation accepted are two different things. Human beings must respond to God's offer, and that response must be, first, to accept the love offered, and, second, to live one's life accordingly, to live out that love in what might be called an "authentic" existence of love.

The grace and demand of God are present realities, not just realities pointing to some distant future "heaven" where we *will* be saved and where our actions then are not needed. The call to love God by loving the neighbor is to be answered at each moment. Salvation is not something gotten and hoarded, some commodity to be stored up against future ills, it is accepted and lived out "new every moment" (as the hymn says).

With regard to the wholism and the this-worldliness demanded by credibility, Jesus' offer of salvation is made in the present, and not just to "souls" but to whole human beings, people of flesh and blood. The call is not a call to be "spiritual" if that means to ignore or despise the body. It is a call to love the neighbor as human being, not the neighbor as disembodied soul. The future is unknown, but the grace of salvation offered allows us to go with trust into that future.

The salvation offered in Jesus is not just between "me and God," for it is a call to love God *through* loving the neighbor, to respond to God in the neighbor. In the twentieth century we recognize that the needs of the neighbor are both caused and met not only by individual circumstances but by social structures that dictate and enforce poverty, sexism, racism, and so forth. We can see that meeting the needs of the neighbor involves large-scale political change as well as individual acts of charity.

Those who appeal to Jesus as example sometimes have trouble at precisely this point, for such an appeal almost invariably means trying to make Jesus the political savior, the reformer of society; yet very little in the Gospel texts would indicate that he saw his role as that of large-scale social reform. I think this desire to make Jesus the political reformer is anachronistic. In Jesus' day (and long thereafter) people were not aware of social structures as humanly created and therefore able to be humanly deposed and re-created. Political power was divine gift and held by divine right. It is only since the Enlightenment that we have been able to see ourselves as the creators of our own social structures. We can hardly ask Jesus not to be a person of his time.

What Jesus calls us to do is to love our neighbor, to meet the needs of the neighbor. The neighbor, of course, is every person. What we need to do in our time and place is to ferret out exactly what this means for us. And we can do this without having to claim that Jesus saw political action in the same way that we do.

Jesus does call for response to God through himself, but most scholars think that the earliest layer of material indicates that he did not make specific claims for himself in terms of titles.[8] Those were attributed to him later. The most exclusive types of claims in the Gospels come from the church's reflections at a later time, for instance the claim that all nations should be baptized at Jesus' command from the end of Matthew's Gospel or the many claims in John's Gospel about Jesus as the only way to God.

The love of God about which Jesus speaks is not the kind of love that can be restricted to the few (or even the many) who come directly in contact with the influence of Jesus. Jesus does not re-present the restriction of God's love but its fullness, its all-encompassing character. He made an urgent call that response to God could take place through him, but nothing in the earliest layer of witness seems to suggest that other ways were definitively ruled out.

Jesus is a ṣavior to whom feminists can relate. He offers a salvation that today requires action for social change, he offers a salvation of the whole human being, of body as well as soul, he offers a this-worldly salvation, and he offers it to all. Feminists do not have to be Christians, but they could be.

Given this sketch of an appropriate and credible christology, how might feminists draw on source material from women's experience to fill in the outlines?

Although we do have a male savior figure in Christianity, we also have source material on which we can draw to lessen its all-male impact. Here I refer to the identification of the Second Person of the Trinity as "Sophia," Lady Wisdom.[9] When we refer not specifically to the Jesus witnessed to in the apostolic tradition but perhaps to the presence of Christ among us, reference to the Second Person of the Trinity as "she" may serve a useful and meaningful function.

Many stories from the Gospels can also give life to this christological outline, to illuminate Jesus' role as the one who re-presents God. Here I do not use these stories as rules: "Jesus did this, we should do likewise." Rather, with these stories we say: "This is the sort of thing that shows forth God's love," and we ask ourselves what it might mean to show that same love in our time and place.

One story from the Gospels that functions as useful source for the feminist theologian is the story of the hemorrhaging woman who touches Jesus' robe (see Matt. 9:20-22; Mark 5:25-34; Luke 8:43-48). Jesus is not appalled because she has polluted him. He praises her faith. From this story we can begin to overcome pollution taboos and to reclaim the goodness of the body. And from the bodily experience they share with this woman, women can attempt new understanding and interpretation of this story. Stories such as this one and the other biblical stories about Jesus and women function as important source material for feminist christology, to develop further an understanding of who Jesus is.

Other stories might be devised. Some might be generated out of scriptural themes—midrash on the biblical texts, appropriate as long as they illumine rather than distort the Jesus of the apostolic witness, credible as long as they do not claim to be something they are not and are not used as vehicles of oppression. Stories might be read forward—what might have happened to Mary Magdalene after the close of the Gospel narrative, for example?

From women's historical experience one can learn about women (such as Sojourner Truth) in whose lives we can see presented yet again the love of God that is centrally re-presented to the Christian in Jesus Christ. With women as the central characters new stories can be written that also render God's love visible. (Here the movie *Babette's Feast* and the story from which it is taken by Karen Blixen under her pen name, Isak Dinesen, come to mind.)

By use of biblical stories, midrash, historical example, and fictional creations feminists can emphasize such themes as wholeness rather than dualism, the goodness of the body, the extension of salvation to all human beings, the social nature of salvation, and the concrete needs of the neighbor. Women's socialized and feminist experiences are essential to interpreting existing traditions and creating new ones. And from such themes a holistic feminist christology can take shape.

Ecclesiology

What does a feminist Christian view of the church look like from the perspective of the criteria of credibility and appropriateness outlined in this book? No church is credible that limits women, calls them inferior, and keeps them as a group from assuming certain roles by speaking of women's role as "different but equal." Nonseparatist feminists recognize that "different but equal" has been a pretext to ban them from certain roles; it is invoked only to keep men in roles that are valued more highly than the roles that are said to be suitable for women. Thus, "different" has come to mean "unequal" to women when they as an entire group are excluded from a role.

Is hierarchical organization in and of itself incredible to the Christian feminist? I would suggest that one needs to define hierarchy before one can answer that question. If hierarchy means that those who have particular gifts and skills exercise these gifts and skills and not others in the service of the church, then, provided this is not used as license to create two or more classes of Christians, it is not inherently inimical to credibility. The problem arises when hierarchy is exclusionary; when it is permanent; when there is no crossover from one "status" to another; and when hierarchy is invoked not just in the area of an individual's expertise but generally to raise an individual's

106

status. Gifts and skills for leadership can be recognized and utilized without excluding the gifts and skills of others.

Of course, any church theology or structure that excludes women as a group from whole areas of the church's life and work (e.g., the clergy) is incredible. Any claims by historical human beings or humanly created structures to be infallible are likewise incredible.

Liturgy is credible if it is used for enriching the whole people of God, but incredible if by language or practice people are excluded from full participation. Liturgy is used as a barrier when its language needlessly fails to take whole parts of the population (women, for instance) into account either by assuming women are included in the pseudo-generic masculine language and appeals to pseudo-generic human experience or by refusal to care whether or not they are included. If there are any roles in the liturgy from which women are, by virtue of their sex, excluded, either officially (as in the refusal of some churches to ordain women to celebrate sacraments) or unofficially (as in some churches' practice of having only male ushers or offering bearers), these liturgical practices are incredible to the feminist.

As I noted in the last section, we now know that human beings create their own social structures and therefore can change them. This is true of the church as well as of other social institutions. The demand for credibility suggests that the organizational structure of any given church has been humanly created and can therefore be humanly altered.

For the feminist it is also incredible to belong to a church that would allow or foster oppression not just within its ranks but also in the broader world. Feminists would not find credible a church that turns only inward to itself and never outward to others.

In the earliest layer of the apostolic witness we certainly cannot find any institution called "church." The one reference to "church" in the Synoptic Gospels (Matt. 16:18) has given rise to a variety of interpretations. Whatever the passage does mean, it does not provide a clear-cut organizational structure.[10] What we do have is a loose-knit group of followers with no particular organization or specific standards for membership. The call to respond, to serve God and neighbor, makes it appropriate that those who hear the call might band together in their response, especially since the call is to life in community, not solitary relationship to God. But certainly there is no one "appropriate" structure or organizational design to follow. No particular structure is either divinely given or dominically instituted. No license is given for claims to infallibility.

Many different church structures might be appropriate as long as they respect the egalitarian nature of the Christian call to response, as long as they embody the salvation extended to all by God's grace through Jesus Christ. Church structure, then, should depend first on embodying the gospel call and message, and second on the particular needs of a given ecclesiastical community, the needs insisted on by credibility. Because of the exigencies of historical existence the church is no longer one church but many. Although this is to be lamented from the point of view of the desire for unity, the different churches, separated by history, now often fulfill different functions and meet different human needs by their tone and character. One can perhaps celebrate the diversity of the church as long as that diversity does not betray either appropriateness or credibility. One may hope that at least some of the diversities can be overcome in a common ground of feminism, which, if embraced, does relativize many of the differences heretofore emphasized, such as those of structure.

As with church structure, so with church leadership no particular form is divinely given or dominically instituted. Again, the appropriate form of leadership is one that promotes the work of the gospel without denying the possibility of full participation for all its members in all its functions. Thus, any form of leadership that meets the needs of the church and serves the interests of the gospel is appropriate. Clearly, as the infant church developed from a charismatic community into an institution, more structure was and continued to be needed, but surely this structure can appropriately take a wide variety of forms.

What is the church for? What should it be doing? The church is the people of God living out their response to God through Jesus Christ. As church, the people of God come together to reflect on, to preach and celebrate, to enact the gospel, the good news of God's grace shown to them in Jesus Christ. The church exists for the mutual support of its members, to meet their needs and so that burdens can be shared rather than borne individually and in solitude. The church also exists to care for the neighbor, both the neighbor within its bounds and the neighbor anywhere in the world.

Of course, the people of God are not limited to those who would explicitly call themselves Christians. Insofar as people might respond to the call of God in other ways than explicitly through the call of God in Jesus Christ, they too are the people of God. A concept of invisible church that extends to them might be helpful from an intra-Christian point of view as long as it is used only as a way for Christians to understand others in Christian terms and not as a way to discount the validity of other religious experiences. Basically, however, I understand "church" as a category that applies to that portion of the people of God who have responded to God through Jesus Christ.

The Christian church does not see itself merely as social institution, for it sees itself as divinely impelled and directed to be a sign (often, admittedly, *the* sign) of God's presence in the world, a sign of the reign of God in the world. In the past the church has, because of some of its stances and actions, often not been a very clear sign of the reign of God. Feminists, for example, can hardly be blamed for not thinking of church as much of a sign of the reign of God if such a sign would mean that all human beings are proclaimed as equal in God's sight. Whether or not it has lived up to its calling, the church does have the capacity and potential to be a sign of God's reign and that ought to be a goal for reform.

The question of ordination is one that many feminists have raised. With regard to appropriateness, the earliest layers of the apostolic tradition contain no concept of ordination, and their concept of leadership is one of charismatic leadership designed to meet the needs of the group.[11] On my understanding of what counts as appropriately Christian, ordination cannot be said to belong to the *esse* or essence of what it means to be church.

It seems to me that from the point of view of credibility, arguments about ordination could be made both ways. One might argue that as long as ordination was not denied to certain groups as groups, it might serve some useful function in a complex church structure. One might argue, conversely, that ordination automatically creates two "classes" of Christians, that it encourages two sets of criteria about acceptable Christian conduct, or the meaning of living out the gospel. Many feminists, Letty Russell, for example, have argued that we need a whole host of models for Christian ministry, not just the traditional model of ordained ministry.[12] Ministry is about sharing one's gifts with the whole community. These gifts may cover a wide range of functions, liturgical, social, educational, and so on. Perhaps ministerial roles should be interchangeable. You take the leadership role or roles for which you have gifts and the community recognizes your gifts and your role. It is worth considering whether or not paid, accountable ministries are needed in the contemporary church, with its size and organizational complexity. Most churches ordain persons in such ministries. Whether to continue this long-standing (even if not strictly "appropriate" by my criteria) custom must be debated by each church in connection with the bounds of appropriateness and credibility and the needs of the individual church.

Liturgies are necessary to celebrate the gospel message and to bring the community together for the worship of the God whose grace sustains them. From the point of view of the criterion of appropriateness, very little can be said about what form that liturgy should take and what its elements should be. There is no early tradition of Jesus baptizing or commanding baptism. The traditions about the Lord's Supper are, in the forms that we have them, also late, reflecting a developed interpretation of the Easter event. Willi Marxsen argues that the earliest tradition in which the Lord's Supper has its roots is the tradition of communal meals, of Jesus eating and drinking with his followers.[13] Thus, according to the criterion of appropriateness found in the earliest layer of witness, the sacraments, although they may be of benefit in edifying the church, are not necessary for the church to be church.

Insofar as the sacraments (or any other liturgical act) proclaim God's grace in the midst of the people, they are appropriate liturgical acts. On the grounds of practical credibility, the sacraments themselves are less likely to come under attack than the rules surrounding who may or may not perform them (the questions of leadership and ordination). Of course, there are many worthy historical sources of liturgical material and many contemporary sources, too, that would embody the rich Christian tradition without excluding any of its members.

With regard to ecclesiology, the earliest layer of apostolic witness gives us very little in terms of the criterion of appropriateness. Therefore, the church must draw on the traditions that have evolved and on its notion of contemporary credibility to forge itself into a viable institution for today.

The structure of the early Christian community as depicted in the Book of Acts is a biblical source that can be put to good use in a feminist ecclesiology, as are the many instances of women as leaders in those early communities. And, as was suggested in connection with christology, the stories of women such as Phoebe and Prisca can be used as the basis of midrash that reflects shared leadership.[14]

There are many women from Christian history whose stories are just beginning to be recovered—women of strength, intelligence, and courage, such as Hildegard of Bingen or Julian of

Norwich, whose leadership made a significant difference to Christian history.[15] Their stories shed light on what it means to be the church in the world. The experience that women have had traditionally as nurturers provides alternative ways to think of leadership, especially when combined with the feminist realization that not only women can learn these roles.

Many feminists are espousing the notion of "women-church."[16] This term does not usually refer to a separate "breakaway" institutional structure. It usually refers to a formally or informally constituted group of women (and sometimes men who share feminist values) meeting as provisional or supplementary church. "Women-church" often sees itself as being one place where, until the whole church is reformed, feminist values can be espoused and agreed upon, where women are treated as equals. Usually members of a women-church community have no desire to start a new institutional church. Usually, in fact, they belong to some institutional church or other (for the most part, they are Roman Catholic, for the movement was begun by Catholic women). But they do want some place to gather as church where women and women's issues are taken seriously, and where women can function as equals in leadership.

Women-church, as long as it is not by definition permanently exclusive, can certainly be seen to be appropriately Christian. And it may be necessary for credibility if one despairs of reforming in the near future the church to which one belongs. It may well be the only credible way for some people to live out the gospel today.

The church has a job to do in the world—the job of proclaiming and living the gospel. It does not need to discount other religious visions to do this, it simply (which is more simply said than done, of course) needs to live up to its own ideals. For the feminist, then, this means first and foremost that the church must be concerned about extending God's love to all God's people by meeting the needs of those people, by seeking to overcome oppression both within the church and outside, by calling and working for all to have a fair and just share of the world's resources. Certainly today one of the rich resources on which a feminist ecclesiology can draw is the example of women living out their Christian commitment in the Third World.

But being the church of Jesus Christ also means celebrating in worship the presence of God through Christ. Such celebration can take many forms, and I think the celebration needs to suit the community in which it is used. I myself favor combining of traditional and contemporary elements. Although I have argued that the Sacraments of Baptism and Eucharist are not essential to the church, I do think they are a powerful way of showing forth God's presence in sign and word.

The imagery of female bodily experience from the medieval period is a source on which feminist preachers and creators of liturgy can draw. New liturgies and sign-acts are being created to mark milestones in women's lives,[17] and such liturgies are appropriately Christian as long as in their celebration they do not lose sight of the presence of God to God's people, for Christians, most centrally in Jesus Christ.

In addition, I think that reflection and study are important elements in being the church today, so we know who we have been as church and who we want to be; so that we know what to repeat from our past because it has led to liberation and what to excise because it has led to oppression.

In whatever ways it can, the church must show forth God's love to the world.

Conclusion

Those who seek to be both Christian theologians and feminist theologians must be willing to enter fully into the meaning of the Christian tradition without compromising their feminist ideals. Yet they accept neither Christian tradition nor feminist ideals uncritically. A Christian feminist theology is forged when one brings to bear on the central Christian claims the concerns of feminists to find a theology that takes women's experience seriously and sees women and men as equals. If women's experience is not taken seriously, theology is incredible in its claims to be *adequate* Christian theology; if the tradition is not taken seriously, theology is inappropriate in its claims to be adequate *Christian* theology.

To do Christian feminist theology, then, requires balance, not the balance of walking a tightrope, afraid to look either way for fear of plunging to death below, but the balance of trying to carry two heavy objects. One must keep shifting the weight in a search for equilibrium. There are various ways in which the weight can be redistributed. The aim is to carry the burden toward one's goal rather than to be so weighted down by it that one cannot move.

EPILOGUE

I am a feminist. I am also committed to remaining within the Christian tradition. I have written this volume in hopes that, by stating my own commitments and showing how I could work them out for myself they might be of use to others engaged with some of the same issues.

In my own life my feminism and my commitment to the institutional church are intertwined. Elisabeth Schüssler Fiorenza has written of the paradox of a tradition that both oppresses and liberates.[1] That, too, has been my experience. I started theological study in the mid-1970s. I entered because I had questions, questions I learned to call "theological" that such study promised to help me ask better, and even, perhaps, to answer, at least for myself. Up to that point I would have said that I had not as a woman experienced sexism.

As I look back on my experience in theological study, I can see that my call to remain in the church and my call to be a feminist were one and the same. In an interview for a summer job, I was asked, "Why don't you give up this stupid idea of being a minister and start learning how to be a good minister's wife?" If I needed "divine intervention," that was it. That experience was the beginning of my ability to see sexism and patriarchy as structural rather than simply as isolated incidents that happened to me and seemed unfair.

Through reading and thought, my understanding of the causes of and alternatives to patriarchy has broadened and deepened. Through the thought of others I have been enabled to see interconnections between the oppression of women and other forms of oppression. The desire to counteract patriarchy is one of the main forces compelling my own theological thought.

My own quest, however, is impelled by other strong forces, too. One of these is the fact that, despite its patriarchy, Christianity is still able to speak to me, to provide a framework for my own religious quest that is meaningful. It seems to speak to other women, too. Many of its symbols, those that I have come to see as central, still are able to answer my religious questions about life's meaning and purpose, about who I am in the universe.

I know that the reason the symbols continue to speak to me is intimately connected to the other strong force that impels my own religious quest. This force is the need for things in my life to make sense, to be coherent, noncontradictory, to be what I have called in this book intellectually credible. As a teenager, I considered leaving the church because I thought it offered only two options: take the whole thing as literally true or leave it. But I was still searching for meaning. During this search I came to undergraduate courses in religious studies, and there I discovered that for scholars there were choices other than "take it or leave it."

In religious studies, and later in theological study, I have always been concerned to come to a position that makes sense both politically and intellectually. In my search, I discovered that Christianity, and religious traditions more generally, could and should be subjected to intellectual query, that there was no question that could not be asked. I also discovered that when one analyzes religious commitment, one discovers that it is far more complex than we are usually taught it is in our Sunday school days. Neither simple acceptance nor simple dismissal of any concept or symbol is possible.

My commitment to Christianity is not a commitment to take it or leave it but a commitment to a Christianity revised and reformed to take many contemporary questions, especially feminist questions, into account. If I came to a point where I thought that such revision was impossible within Christian commitment, I would leave.

It is because I think it possible to be a feminist and a Christian that I stay within the Christian church. I do not think it easy to be both feminist and Christian. To make a commitment to be part of religious tradition is, it seems to me, to make a decision on at least three fronts. First, it has to make political sense. It has to allow for the possibility of an analysis of the political and social situations and relations one encounters in the world, and it has to be able to provide a means of criticism for what exists and an envisaging of alternatives. Although I do not think that Christianity is the only means by which such analysis is done, I do think that it is open to various means of political and social analysis, and I do think that its vision is one that can be used by women as they seek to work out their political and social future.

Second, it has to make intellectual sense, to be able to account for the way the world is and is experienced. I do think that it is possible to understand and interpret the central concepts and symbols of Christianity in such a way that they give as adequate an account as possible of the way the world is in most general terms (that is, Christianity can provide an adequate metaphysics); and they give me some way to understand my presence as a woman within that world. Admittedly this requires much revision and rethinking of traditional categories, but it does not, I think, require abandoning the tradition.

Third, the tradition has to have what, for lack of a better word, I will call aesthetic appeal for its adherents. It has to "feel" right to them. It has to be able in its liturgies or rituals to embody the meaning they find there. Clearly here is a front where Christianity has much still to do for feminists. Once the symbols have been revised and reinterpreted, they need to be put to feminist use.

Whether and how to continue to claim Christianity is a problem for many feminists. It is not easily resolved by providing a checklist and saying, "If you affirm x number of things on this list you should stay (or leave)." The decision to stay or leave is a very personal one. I have not attempted in this book to say that all should stay because Christianity is a religious tradition ideally suited to feminist needs. It is not. What I have attempted to say is that, if the complex of needs I describe here rings true for others, then perhaps Christianity can still offer possibilities for some religious feminists.

I have explored my place and calling in the world beginning with explicit feminist commitments, recognizing the structural forms of patriarchy that stunt women's intellectual, spiritual, and social growth into full humanity. I remain committed to seeing all women grow to that fullness by whatever means are necessary. For me, that place and calling are illumined by thinking in categories that partake of the political sphere and yet transcend it. Christian theology has provided those categories, and I have been able to find ways to revise those categories that seem (to me, at least, though surely not to all) to allow the possibility of overcoming patriarchal bias. Theology, as second-order reflection, has been the way that I have entered my own religious quest.

I am aware that theology, by itself, will not change women's lives. Other analyses must be given; courses of action must be followed. Yet I enter into the discussion where I am equipped to do so. Others enter the discussion in other places. What we cannot do singly we may do together—both in theory and in practice to work for a world in which the full humanity of women is realized.

NOTES

1/THE FEMINIST CHALLENGE AND THEOLOGICAL METHOD

1. Rosemary Radford Ruether, "The Future of Feminist Theology in the Academy," *Journal of the American Academy of Religion* 53 (1985): 703–13.

2. See, e.g., Lorraine Code, "Feminist Theory," in Sandra Burt, Lorraine Code, and Lindsay Dorney, eds., *Changing Patterns: Women in Canada* (Toronto: McClelland and Stewart, 1988), 18–50.

3. Some examples of works from this first stage are: Mary Daly, *The Church and the Second Sex* (New York: Harper and Row, 1975); Alice L. Hageman, ed., *Sexist Religion and Women in the Church: No More Silence!* (New York: Association, 1974); Rosemary Radford Ruether, ed., *Religion and Sexism: Images of Woman in the Jewish and Christian Traditions* (New York: Simon and Schuster, 1974); Letty Russell, ed., *The Liberating Word: A Guide to Nonsexist Interpretation of the Bible* (Philadelphia: Westminster, 1976).

4. Tertullian *On the Apparel of Women*, chap. 1; Thomas Aquinas, *Summa Theologica*, Part I, Question 92.

5. Some examples of works from this second stage are: Anne E. Carr, *Transforming Grace: Christian Tradition and Women's Experience* (San Francisco: Harper and Row, 1988); Mary Daly, *Beyond God the Father: Toward a Philosophy of Women's Liberation* (Boston: Beacon, 1973); Elisabeth Schüssler Fiorenza, *In Memory of Her: A Feminist Theological Reconstruction of Christian Origins* (New York: Crossroad, 1983); Elisabeth Moltmann-Wendel, *A Land Flowing with Milk and Honey: Perspectives on Feminist Theology*, trans. John Bowden (New York: Crossroad, 1986); Rosemary Radford Ruether, *Sexism and God-Talk: Toward a Feminist Theology* (Boston: Beacon, 1983); Rosemary Radford Ruether and Eleanor McLaughlin, eds., *Women of Spirit: Female Leadership in the Jewish and Christian Traditions* (New York: Simon and Schuster, 1979); Letty Russell, *Human Liberation in a Feminist Perspective: A Theology* (Philadelphia: Westminster, 1974); Phyllis Trible, *God and the Rhetoric of Sexuality* (Philadelphia: Fortress, 1978).

6. See, e.g., Sallie McFague, *Models of God: Theology for an Ecological, Nuclear Age* (Philadelphia: Fortress, 1987).

7. See, e.g., Letty Russell, *The Future of Partnership* (Philadelphia: Westminster, 1979), 121–39; or Rosemary Radford Ruether, *Women-Church: Theology and Practice* (San Francisco: Harper and Row, 1985), 11–95.

8. See, e.g., Mary Malone, "A Time for Mary Magdalene: Prostitution or Proclamation?" in Michael W. Higgins and Douglas R. Letson, eds., *Women and the Church: A Sourcebook* (Toronto: Griffin House, 1986), 105–8; or Elisabeth Schüssler Fiorenza, "Feminist Theology as a Critical Theology of Liberation," in Gerald H. Anderson and Thomas F. Stransky, eds., *Mission Trends*

No. 4: Liberation Theologies in North America and Europe (New York: Paulist, 1979), 209–11.

9. See, e.g., Elisabeth Schüssler Fiorenza, "Women in the Early Christian Movement," in Carol Christ and Judith Plaskow, eds., *Womanspirit Rising* (San Francisco: Harper and Row, 1979), 90; or Barbara J. MacHaffie, *Her Story: Women in Christian Tradition* (Philadelphia: Fortress, 1986), 25, 109.

10. Daly, *Beyond God the Father*, 11.

11. Ibid.

12. See, e.g., Letty Russell, ed., *Feminist Interpretation of the Bible* (Philadelphia: Westminster, 1985); and Adela Yarbro Collins, ed., *Feminist Perspectives on Biblical Scholarship* (Chico: Scholars Press, 1985). Both books contain essays by other scholars who might fit into one of the methodological positions I outline and provide examples of other ways to classify feminist methodologies.

2/SOME FEMINIST METHODOLOGIES

1. Some other feminist theologians who, despite their differences from Schüssler Fiorenza, would seem to fit into this first category are: Rita Nakashima Brock, Claudia Camp, and Phyllis Trible.

2. In a few places in her early feminist work, Schüssler Fiorenza wrote of the need for a Christian feminist theology to show that Christian faith and church are not inherently sexist, but she then made the methodological move to her present position that one cannot say anything about what is inherent to Christianity. See, e.g., "Feminist Theology as a Critical Theology of Liberation," in Gerald H. Anderson and Thomas F. Stransky, eds., *Mission Trends 4: Liberation Theologies in North America and Europe* (New York: Paulist, 1979), 203.

3. Elisabeth Schüssler Fiorenza, *In Memory of Her: A Feminist Theological Reconstruction of Christian Origins* (New York: Crossroad, 1983), 32.

4. Elisabeth Schüssler Fiorenza, *Bread Not Stone: The Challenge of Feminist Biblical Interpretation* (Boston: Beacon, 1984), 14.

5. Ibid., 86.

6. Elisabeth Schüssler Fiorenza, "Toward a Feminist Biblical Hermeneutics: Biblical Interpretation and Liberation Theology," in Brian Mahan and L. Dale Richesin, eds., *The Challenge of Liberation Theology: A First World Response* (Maryknoll, N.Y.: Orbis, 1984), 108; see also Schüssler Fiorenza, *Bread Not Stone*, 40–41.

7. Elisabeth Schüssler Fiorenza, "The Will to Choose or to Reject: Continuing Our Critical Work," in Letty Russell, ed., *Feminist Interpretation of the Bible* (Philadelphia: Westminster, 1985), 131.

8. Ibid., 126.

9. Ibid., 128.

10. Ibid., 126.

11. See, e.g., Schüssler Fiorenza, *In Memory of Her*, 32–33; and *Bread Not Stone*, 61.

12. Elisabeth Schüssler Fiorenza, "Emerging Issues in Feminist Biblical Interpretation," in Judith Weidman, ed., *Christian Feminism: Visions of a New Humanity* (San Francisco: Harper and Row, 1984), 35–36; see also *Bread Not Stone*, xxiv, 3.

13. See, e.g., Schüssler Fiorenza, *Bread Not Stone*, 28f.

14. See, e.g., ibid., 84.

15. Schüssler Fiorenza, *In Memory of Her*, xix.

16. Schüssler Fiorenza, *Bread Not Stone*, 53

17. Schüssler Fiorenza, "The Will to Choose or to Reject," 126.

18. Schüssler Fiorenza, "Emerging Issues," 46; see also *Bread Not Stone*, 14, 40.

19. See, e.g., Schüssler Fiorenza, *Bread Not Stone*, xvi.

20. See, e.g., Schüssler Fiorenza, "Emerging Issues," and also *Bread Not Stone*, 15-18, 21, 108, 148.

21. See, e.g., Schüssler Fiorenza, *In Memory of Her*, 121.

22. See Schüssler Fiorenza, "The Will to Choose or to Reject," 126.

23. Elisabeth Schüssler Fiorenza, "Claiming the Center: A Critical Feminist Theology of Liberation," in Janet Kalven and Mary J. Buckley, eds., *Women's Spirit Bonding* (New York: Pilgrim, 1984), 307.

24. Schüssler Fiorenza, *Bread Not Stone*, 49.

25. Some other feminist theologians who, despite their differences from Ruether, would seem to fit into this second category are: Sheila Collins, Sharon Ringe, Delores S. Williams.

26. Rosemary Radford Ruether, "The Future of Feminist Theology in the Academy," *Journal of the American Academy of Religion* 53 (1985): 709.

27. Rosemary Radford Ruether, *Sexism and God-Talk: Toward a Feminist Theology* (Boston: Beacon: 1983), 18–19.

28. Ibid., 19.

29. Ibid., 21–22.

30. Rosemary Radford Ruether, "Feminist Spirituality and Historical Religion," *Harvard Divinity Bulletin* 16, 3 (1986): 11.

31. Rosemary Radford Ruether, "Feminist Theology: What It Is, Why It Is Necessary," *Unitarian Universalist World* 17, 7 (September, 1986): 8.

32. Ibid.

33. Ruether, "The Future of Feminist Theology," 710.

34. Ibid., 711.

35. In her first book, *The Church against Itself* (New York: Herder and Herder, 1967), Ruether gave final normative say to the individual in encounter with the Holy Spirit. See 119, 226.

36. Ruether, *Sexism and God-Talk*, 15–16.

37. Rosemary Radford Ruether, *Womanguides* (Boston: Beacon, 1985), xi.

38. Ruether, "Feminist Theology: What It Is," 8.

39. For the development of the term "women-church" see Rosemary Radford Ruether, *Women-Church: Theology and Practice* (San Francisco: Harper and Row, 1985), 283, n. 4; see also Schüssler Fiorenza, *Bread Not Stone*, 1–22; and

Anne E. Carr, *Transforming Grace: Christian Tradition and Women's Experience* (San Francisco: Harper and Row, 1988), 200, 210.

40. Rosemary Radford Ruether in James M. Wall, ed., *Theologians in Transition* (New York: Crossroad, 1981), 164.

41. Ruether, *Sexism and God-Talk*, 24.

42. See, e.g., Rosemary Radford Ruether, "A Religion for Women: Sources and Strategies," *Christianity and Crisis* 39, 119 (1979): 309.

43. Rosemary Radford Ruether, *To Change the World: Christology and Cultural Criticism* (New York: Crossroad, 1981), 3.

44. Ibid.

45. Ruether, *Sexism and God-Talk*, 135.

46. Ruether, *To Change the World*, 5.

47. Ruether, *Sexism and God-Talk*, 213.

48. Some other feminist theologians who, despite their differences from Russell, would seem to fit into this third category are: Anne E. Carr, Virginia Ramey Mollenkott, Elisabeth Moltmann-Wendel, Patricia Wilson-Kastner.

49. Letty Russell, *Human Liberation in a Feminist Perspective: A Theology* (Philadelphia: Westminster, 1974), 52; see also Letty Russell, *The Future of Partnership* (Philadelphia: Westminster, 1979), 142.

50. See, e.g., Russell, *Human Liberation*.

51. Letty Russell, "Beginning from the Other End," *Duke Divinity School Review* 45 (1980): 100.

52. Russell, *Human Liberation*, 40.

53. Letty Russell, *Household of Freedom: Authority in Feminist Theology* (Philadelphia: Westminster, 1987), 23.

54. Russell, *Human Liberation*, 53.

55. Russell, "Beginning from the Other End," 103.

56. Russell, *Household of Freedom*, 18.

57. Letty Russell, "Authority and the Challenge of Feminist Interpretation," in Letty Russell, ed., *Feminist Interpretation of the Bible* (Philadelphia: Westminster, 1985), 140.

58. It should be made clear that although I am concentrating on the feminist aspect of Russell's critique, she means for the critique to serve any oppressed group.

59. Russell, "Authority and the Challenge of Feminist Interpretation," 140–41.

60. Russell, *Human Liberation*, 78. On the subject of "usable past" see Eleanor McLaughlin, "The Christian Past: Does It Hold a Future for Women?" in Carol Christ and Judith Plaskow, eds., *Womanspirit Rising* (San Francisco: Harper and Row, 1979), 94–95.

61. See, e.g., Russell, *Human Liberation*, 96ff.

62. Russell, *Household of Freedom*, 53.

63. Ibid., 47.

64. Russell, "Authority and the Challenge of Feminist Interpretation," 144.

65. Russell, *Household of Freedom*, 35.

66. Letty Russell, "Inclusive Language and Power," *Religious Education* 80 (1985): 590.

67. Russell, *Human Liberation*, 58.

68. Russell, *Household of Freedom*, 23.

69. Russell, "Beginning from the Other End," 104.

70. Russell, *The Future of Partnership*, 44.

71. See, e.g., ibid., 22.

72. Russell, "Beginning from the Other End," 101.

73. Russell, "Authority and the Challenge of Feminist Interpretation," 139.

74. Russell, "Beginning from the Other End," 105.

75. Russell, *The Future of Partnership*, 53.

76. Russell, *Household of Freedom*, 20.

77. Russell, "Beginning from the Other End," 98; see also her "Authority and the Challenge of Feminist Interpretation," 138.

78. Russell, "Authority and the Challenge of Feminist Interpretation," 141.

79. Ibid., 146.

3/WOMEN'S EXPERIENCE AS SOURCE AND NORM OF THEOLOGY

1. Some feminists who discuss women's experience are Rebecca Chopp, "Feminism's Theological Pragmatics: A Social Naturalism of Women's Experience," *Journal of Religion* 67 (1987): 239–56; Judith Plaskow, *Sex, Sin and Grace* (Washington, D.C.: University Press of America, 1980), 29–48; Letty Russell, *Household of Freedom* (Philadelphia: Westminster, 1987), 18; Rosemary Radford Ruether, "Feminist Theology: What It Is, Why It Is Necessary," *Unitarian Universalist World* 17, 7 (September 1986): 8; Elisabeth Schüssler Fiorenza, *In Memory of Her* (New York: Crossroad, 1983), 32.

2. Alfred North Whitehead, *Modes of Thought* (New York: The Free Press, 1968), 116.

3. Penelope Washbourn, *Becoming Woman* (New York: Harper and Row, 1977), 3.

4. Mary Daly, *Beyond God the Father* (Boston: Beacon, 1973), 8.

5. Many works could be cited. Here I will give just a few examples. Mary Daly, *The Church and the Second Sex* (Boston: Beacon, 1968); Jean Baker Miller, *Towards a New Psychology of Women* (Boston: Beacon, 1976); Sheila Rowbotham, *Woman's Consciousness, Man's World* (New York: Penguin, 1973); Anne Wilson Schaef, *Women's Reality* (Minneapolis: Winston, 1981).

6. See, e.g., Valerie Saiving, "The Human Situation: A Feminine View," in Carol Christ and Judith Plaskow, eds., *Womanspirit Rising* (San Francisco: Harper and Row, 1979), 25–42.

7. Plaskow, *Sex, Sin and Grace*, 11.

8. See, e.g., Letty Russell, *Human Liberation in a Feminist Perspective: A Theology* (Philadelphia: Westminster, 1974), 55; or Juan Luis Segundo, *The Liberation of Theology* (New York: Orbis, 1979), 81ff. The criticism employed

here of liberation theology's definition of theology is developed by Schubert M. Odgen in *Faith and Freedom* (Nashville: Abingdon, 1979) and in "The Concept of a Theology of Liberation: Must a Christian Theology Today Be So Conceived?" in Brian Mahan and L. Dale Richesin, eds., *The Challenge of Liberation Theology: A First World Response* (Maryknoll, N.Y.: Orbis, 1984), 127–40.

9. The notion of theology as fully critical and fully reflective comes from Schubert M. Ogden. See, e.g., "What is Theology?" *Journal of Religion* 52 (1972): 22–40.

10. In *Models of God* (Philadelphia: Fortress, 1987), 40–41, Sallie McFague argues, following David Tracy, that these two "givens" or "constants" are foundational for "most recognizably Christian theologies, because of a peculiarity of Christian religion: its claim to be both historical and contemporary."

11. See Eleanor McLaughlin, "The Christian Past: Does It Hold a Future for Women?" in Christ and Plaskow, eds., *Womanspirit Rising*, 93–106.

12. See, e.g., Rosemary Radford Ruether, *Womanguides*, (Boston: Beacon, 1985).

13. Two theologians whose work has influenced my understanding of credibility are Schubert M. Ogden (see, e.g., his *On Theology* [San Francisco: Harper and Row, 1986]) and Charles M. Wood (see, e.g., his *Vision and Discernment* [Atlanta: Scholars Press, 1985]).

14. See, Saiving, "The Human Situation," and Plaskow, *Sex, Sin and Grace*.

15. For a good discussion of inclusive language see Pamela J. Milne, "Women and Words: The Use of Non-Sexist, Inclusive Language in the Academy," *Studies in Religion/Sciences Religieuses* 18/1 (1989): 25–35.

16. The person who has best detailed these dualisms is Rosemary Radford Ruether. See, e.g., her *New Woman/New Earth* (New York: Seabury, 1975).

4/THE PLACE OF CHRISTIAN TRADITION IN A CHRISTIAN FEMINIST THEOLOGY

1. Letty Russell, "Beginning from the Other End," *Duke Divinity School Review* 45 (1980): 101.

2. Elaine Pagels, *The Gnostic Gospels* (New York: Random House, 1979), 70–83.

3. See, e.g., Eleanor McLaughlin, "The Christian Past: Does It Hold a Future for Women?" in Carol Christ and Judith Plaskow, eds., *Womanspirit Rising* (San Francisco: Harper and Row, 1979), 93–106.

4. Schubert M. Ogden discusses the term "appropriateness" in many places. See, e.g., his "What Is Theology?" *Journal of Religion* 52 (1972): 25.

5. Peter Slater, *The Dynamics of Religion* (San Francisco: Harper and Row, 1978), 28.

6. Ibid., 30.

7. Ibid., 33–34.

8. Ibid., 34.

9. Tom Driver, *Christ in a Changing World* (New York: Crossroad, 1981).

10. Ibid., 143

11. See, e.g., Ruether in James M. Wall, ed., *Theologians in Transition* (New York: Crossroad, 1981), 164.

12. *New Catholic Encyclopedia*, s.v. "Teaching Authority of the Church (Magisterium)."

13. See, e.g., T. Howland Sanks, *Authority in the Church: A Study in Changing Paradigms* (Missoula, Mont.: Scholars Press, 1974), and George H. Tavard, *Holy Writ or Holy Church* (New York: Harper and Row, 1959).

14. Here I am taking up a criticism suggested by Schubert M. Ogden in an unpublished paper, "Women and the Canon: Some Thoughts on the Significance of Rudolf Bultmann's Theology Today."

15. Schubert M. Ogden, *The Point of Christology* (San Francisco: Harper and Row, 1982), 102–3.

16. See, e.g., Günther Bornkamm, *Jesus of Nazareth*, trans. Irene and Fraser McLuskey with James M. Robinson (London: Hodder and Stoughton, 1960); Herbert Braun, *Jesus of Nazareth: the Man and His Time*, trans. Everett R. Kalin (Philadelphia: Fortress, 1979); Martin Dibelius, *Jesus*, trans. Charles B. Hedrick and Frederick Grant (Philadelphia: Westminster, 1949); Willi Marxsen "Christology in the New Testament," *Interpreter's Dictionary of the Bible: Supplementary Volume* (Nashville: Abingdon, 1976), 146–56; Pheme Perkins, *Reading the New Testament: An Introduction*, 2nd ed. (New York: Paulist, 1988), 78–89; E. P. Sanders, *Jesus and Judaism* (Philadelphia: Fortress, 1985); Elisabeth Schüssler Fiorenza, *In Memory of Her: A Feminist Theological Reconstruction of Christian Origins* (New York: Crossroad, 1983), 118ff.

17. Braun, *Jesus of Nazareth*, 42.

18. Marxsen, "Christology in the New Testament," 147.

19. Marxsen, ibid., 146–47; Braun, *Jesus of Nazareth*, 25.

20. See, e.g., Sanders, *Jesus and Judaism*, 325.

21. Pheme Perkins, "God in the New Testament: Preliminary Soundings," *Theology Today* 42 (1985): 334.

22. Ibid., 335.

23. Dibelius, *Jesus*, 103.

24. Marxsen, "Christology in the New Testament," 147.

25. See, e.g., Sanders, *Jesus and Judaism*, 323; or Pheme Perkins, "Women in the Bible and its World," *Interpretation* 42 (1988): 44.

26. John Dominic Crossan, "Divine Immediacy and Human Immediacy: Towards a New First Principle in Historical Jesus Research," *Semeia* 44 (1988): 125.

27. Ibid., 125–6.

5/THE METHOD ENACTED: CHRIST AND CHURCH

1. "Vatican Declaration: Women in the Ministerial Priesthood," *Origins* 6, 33 (1977): 522.

2. Ibid.

3. Ibid.

4. Mary Daly, *Beyond God the Father* (Boston: Beacon, 1973), 19.

5. Rudolf Bultmann, "New Testament and Mythology," in Bultmann, *New Testament and Mythology and Other Basic Writings,* selected, edited, and translated by Schubert M. Ogden (Philadelphia: Fortress, 1984), 2ff.

6. "Objectification" is used by Karl Rahner. See, e.g., his *Foundations of Christian Faith*, trans. William V. Dych (New York: Seabury, 1978), 153ff.

7. Schubert M. Ogden uses the term "re-presentation" to indicate how Jesus presents *again* what we already as human beings know of God implicitly. See, e.g., his *Point of Christology* (San Francisco: Harper and Row, 1982), 76.

8. See, e.g., Reginald Fuller and Pheme Perkins, *Who Is This Christ? Gospel Christology and Contemporary Faith* (Philadelphia: Fortress, 1983), 41–50; Willi Marxsen, *The Beginnings of Christology*, trans. Paul J. Achtemeier and Lorenz Nieting (Philadelphia: Fortress, 1979), 38ff.; E. P. Sanders, *Jesus and Judaism* (Philadelphia: Fortress, 1985), 321–22, 324–25; Eduard Schweizer, *Jesus*, trans. David E. Green (Atlanta: John Knox, 1971), 13–22.

9. For a good treatment of the Second Person of the Trinity as Sophia, see Elizabeth A. Johnson, "Jesus, The Wisdom of God: A Biblical Basis for Non-Androcentric Christology," *Ephemerides Theologicae Lovanianses* 61, 4 (1985): 261–94.

10. For further reading see Dennis C. Duling, "Binding and Loosing: Matthew 16:19; Matthew 18:18; John 20:23," *Forum* 3, 4 (1987): 3–31; and K. L. Schmidt, "ἐκκλησία," in Gerhard Kittel, ed., *Theological Dictionary of the New Testament*, Vol. 3, (Grand Rapids: Eerdman's, 1965), 504, 518–26.

11. See, e.g., Elisabeth Schüssler Fiorenza, *In Memory of Her: A Feminist Theological Reconstruction of Christian Origins* (New York: Crossroad, 1983), 130–54; Xavier Léon-Dufour, *Dictionary of the New Testament*, trans. Terrence Prendergast (San Francisco: Harper and Row, 1980), 290–91; *Oxford Dictionary of the Christian Church*, s.v. "Orders and Ordination."

12. See, e.g., Letty Russell, *The Future of Partnership* (Philadelphia: Westminster, 1979), 121–39.

13. Willi Marxsen, *The Beginnings of Christology*, 69–76.

14. On Phoebe and Prisca see, Elisabeth Schüssler Fiorenza, "Word, Spirit and Power: Women in Early Christian Communities," in Rosemary Radford Ruether and Eleanor McLaughlin, eds., *Women of Spirit* (New York: Simon and Schuster, 1979), 32–36; see also a contemporary letter by "Phoebe" in Elisabeth Schüssler Fiorenza, *In Memory of Her*, 61–64.

15. See Julian of Norwich, *Revelations of Divine Love* (London: Methuen, 1901); Julian of Norwich, *Showings*, trans. and intr. Edmund Colledge and James Walsh (New York: Paulist, 1978); on Julian of Norwich see, Eleanor McLaughlin, "The Christian Past: Does It Hold A Future for Women?" in Carol Christ and Judith Plaskow, eds., *Womanspirit Rising* (San Francisco: Harper and Row, 1979), 101–5. See Hildegard of Bingen, *Illuminations of Hildegard*

Bingen (Santa Fe: Bear and Co., 1985); Hildegard of Bingen, *Scivias* (Santa Fe: Bear and Co., 1986); on Hildegard of Bingen, see Barbara Newman, *Sister of Wisdom: St. Hildegard's Theology of the Feminine* (Berkeley: University of California Press, 1987).

16. On the topic of "women-church" see Rosemary Radford Ruether, *Women-Church* (San Francisco: Harper and Row, 1985), especially 57ff.; and Elisabeth Schüssler Fiorenza, *In Memory of Her* (New York: Crossroad, 1983), especially, 343ff.

17. See, e.g., Rosemary Radford Ruether, *Women-Church*, 122–282.

EPILOGUE

1. Elisabeth Schüssler Fiorenza, "Feminist Spirituality, Christian Identity, and Catholic Vision," in Carol Christ and Judith Plaskow, eds., *Womanspirit Rising* (San Francisco: Harper and Row, 1979), 136–48.

INDEX

Androcentrism, androcentric, 25, 27, 29, 35, 43
Anti-Semitic, anti-Semitism, 39, 88
Apocalyptic, 86
Apostolicity, apostolic witness, apostolic tradition, 39, 84–85, 87, 101, 104, 107
Appropriate, 31, 73, 104, 108–10, 112
Appropriateness, 73–76, 85, 90–92, 95, 101, 106, 110–11, 124
Authority, 42–44, 48, 68–69, 80, 85, 96
Bible, 24–29, 37–38, 44, 46, 79, 82, 88
Biblical androcentric tradition, 25
Biblical interpretation, 26
Biblical liberating tradition, 34
Biblical witness, 25, 37–38, 88
Braun, H., 86, 125
Brock, R. N., 120
Bultmann, R., 98, 126
Camp, C., 120
Canon, 25–26, 29, 35–36, 84–85, 125
Carr, A. E., 119, 122
Christ, 22, 31, 39, 78–80, 83, 104–5
  Jesus as, 33, 39–41, 43–47, 78–80, 83, 88–89, 96–97, 105, 108–9, 113
Christian, Christians, 7, 20–22, 25–29, 33–35, 37–38, 40–41, 43–44, 46–48, 52, 57–65, 67–69, 71–72, 74–81, 88, 92–95, 98–99, 101–2, 104, 106, 108–118
Christian tradition, 7–8, 12, 20–23, 31–35, 40, 43, 48, 62, 69, 71–75, 80, 88, 113, 115
Christianity, 7, 13, 24, 28, 34–35, 38, 80–81, 83–84, 88, 91, 96, 104, 116–18
Christology, 38, 93, 95–106, 111
Church, 7–8, 13–14, 16, 22, 27, 31, 34, 36, 39, 41, 44–45, 61, 69, 71–72, 74–75, 81–82, 92, 95, 97, 100, 106–18, 121, 123, 125
  leadership in the church, 95, 108, 111
Collins, S., 121
Consciousness, 50
Credibility, 22, 62–65, 73–76, 91–97, 100, 104, 106–8, 110–12, 124
  intellectual credibility, 63, 68, 76, 95–97, 116
  practical credibility, 64–65, 76, 111
Crossan, J. D., 88, 125
Culture, 15–16
Daly, M., 17, 54, 96–97, 119–20, 123, 126
Dibelius, M., 87, 125
Dinesen, I., 105
Doctrine, 14
Driver, T., 79, 125
Dualism, 25, 66, 106, 124
Duling, D., 126
Ecclesiology, 93, 106–14
Eclecticism, 24
  feminist, 21, 24, 31
  practical, 33, 69
Ecumenism
  feminist, 33, 79
Eve, 12–14, 16
Example, *exemplum*, 44, 46, 87, 89, 101–3
Experience, 8, 19, 22, 40–41, 43, 46, 49–57, 66–68, 87, 99, 115
  as knowledge, 49–50
  as meaning, 50–51
  nonsensuous, 50–51, 53
  of God, 51, 66
  religious, 52
  through senses, 50–51

See also Men's experience; Women's experience

Faith, 14, 25, 29–30, 37, 43, 46–48, 57–59, 64, 66, 68, 72, 83–84, 86, 105

Feminism, 7–8, 78, 108, 115

Feminist, Feminists, 7–8, 11–18, 20–21, 23–24, 26, 28–29, 31–35, 37, 40–43, 48–49, 52–53, 56, 59, 60–61, 63, 65, 67–69, 71, 73–76, 78–82, 90–97, 100–1, 104–7, 109–18, 123

Feminist theology; See Theology

Fuller, R., 126

Gnostic texts, 72

God, 13–15, 30–31, 37–40, 42, 44–48, 51–52, 57, 77, 79, 84, 86–91, 96–99, 101–5, 109, 112

names and images for, 42, 51

Father, 77, 101–2

Gospel, 38, 44, 82–84, 86, 88–91, 101–5, 107–10, 112, 126

Grace, 26, 30, 87, 98–99, 100, 102–3, 108–111, 119, 123

Hageman, A. L., 119

Hermeneutics, 25, 29–30, 46

Hierarchy, 14, 27, 43–44, 106

Hildegard of Bingen, 111, 126–127

History, 12–14, 17, 28, 30–31, 33, 35, 40–41, 61, 73, 100, 108, 112

women's, 12–14, 17, 21, 28, 42, 56, 61, 72

Historical criticism, 83–85

Incarnation, 97

Infallibility, 108

Jesus, 20, 24, 30, 33, 37–39, 44–47, 72, 78–80, 83–90, 96–106

as re-presentation of God, 99, 101, 104–5, 126

maleness of, 38, 90, 96–101

Jesus movement, 72

Judaism, 34, 39, 76, 125–26

Julian of Norwich, 111–12, 126

Junia, 16

Kelsey, D., 47

Léon-Dufour, X., 126

Liberation, 25–6, 28–31, 39–40, 44–47, 57, 62, 81, 91, 113

Liturgy, liturgical, 14, 29, 106–7, 110–11, 113

Love

God's, 15, 44, 86–87, 90–91, 99, 102–5, 112–13

human, 86–87, 91, 102–5

Luther, M., 82–83

MacHaffie, B. J., 120

Magisterium, 20–21, 23, 26, 80–83

of Pope and bishops, 80–83

of women-church or of women's experience, 21, 23–31, 81–82

Male savior figure, 96–101, 104

Malone, M., 119

Man, men, 15, 54, 57, 60–61, 65–66, 97

Marxsen, W., 86–87, 111, 125–26

Mary, 14

Mary Magdalene, 16, 105, 119

McFague, S., 119, 124

McLaughlin, E., 60, 72, 119, 122, 124, 126

Meaning, 51, 66, 100, 116

Men's experience, 52

Messiah, 38, 86, 88–89, 102

Method, methodology, 7–8, 11, 17–24, 31–32, 43, 94–95

Methodolatry, 17

Midrash, 34, 104–5, 111

Milne, P. J., 124

Ministry, 14, 110–11

Mollenkott, V. R., 122

Moltmann-Wendel, E., 119, 122

Newman, B., 127

Non-persons, 46, 62, 64

Norm of theology, 11, 19–27, 29–32, 35–38, 40–41, 43, 49, 62–67, 69, 71, 73–93, 95, 101

Normative, 27, 30, 33, 35, 45, 73–74, 79–80, 82, 84, 87, 90, 97

Ogden, S. M., 84–85, 124–26

Oppression, 7, 11–12, 14, 25–31, 36–

37, 39, 42, 46, 59–60, 62, 64, 79, 99–100, 107, 113–15
  of women, 7, 11–12, 21, 25–26, 31, 68
Oppressed, 13, 47, 74, 81
Ordination, 13–14, 110–11
  of women, 97, 107
Pagels, E., 72, 124
Particularity, 79
Patriarchal theology, 11, 15, 67
Patriarchy, patriarchal, 12, 15–18, 25–27, 29, 33–36, 39, 42, 61, 67, 75, 77, 90–92, 99, 115–16, 118
Perkins, P., 87, 125–26
Phoebe, 111, 126
Plaskow, J., 56, 65, 120, 122–24, 126–27
Pope, 20, 80, 82
Praxis, 40, 57–58
Preferential option for the poor, 25
Priest, 97
Prisca, 111, 126
Prophetic-liberating theme, 37, 88
Prophetic-liberating tradition, 24, 35, 37, 79, 88
Radical conversion, 77
Reconstruction of theology, 12–14
Reformers, 82, 84
Reign of God, 38, 86–87, 109–10
Religion, 11, 25–26, 31–32, 34, 37, 41, 75, 78, 121–22, 124
Religious quest, 25, 116, 118
Religious tradition, 75–79, 89, 116–18
Revelation, revelatory, 25–29, 35, 39, 44, 98–99, 101
Ringe, S., 121
Ritual, 117
Ruether, R. R., 8, 11, 22, 24, 27, 31–40, 49, 59, 67–69, 71, 74, 76, 79, 88–89, 119, 121–27
Russell, L., 8, 22, 24, 27, 40–47, 49, 59, 67–68, 72, 88–89, 110, 119–20, 122–24, 126
Sacrament, *sacramentum*, sacraments, 87, 89, 102, 107, 111, 113

Saiving, V., 65, 123–24
Salvation, 16, 29, 99–104, 106
Sanders, E. P., 125–26
Schmidt, K. L., 126
Schüssler Fiorenza, E., 8, 22, 24–31, 40, 49, 59, 67–69, 72, 74, 81, 115, 120, 121, 123, 125–27
Schweizer, E., 126
Scripture, 15, 17, 20, 27–31, 34–35, 37–38, 41, 43–48, 62, 71–72, 75, 80–82, 88
Sin, 16, 65–66, 100
Slater, P., 76–78, 124
Social structures, societal structures, 26, 91, 99–100, 103–4, 107
Sola Scriptura, 21, 82
Sophia, 104
Source of theology, 19–20, 22–23, 31–35, 38, 48–49, 53, 56, 60–62, 64, 67–68, 71–73, 76, 82, 85, 95, 104–5, 111
Symbol, 7, 33, 35–37, 76–80, 83, 116–17
  primary, 76–78
  central, 76–80
Synoptic tradition, 101
Tertullian, 13, 119
Theologian, 11, 13–14, 16–18, 23, 31–33, 40–41, 44, 65, 73–74, 76, 78, 113
Theology, 8, 11–13, 15–26, 28–33, 35–41, 43–44, 47–49, 52–68, 72–76, 79–82, 84, 92–95, 107, 114, 118, 120, 124
  Christian, 7–8, 15–16, 18, 20–21, 24, 28, 30, 32–34, 40–41, 44, 48, 52–53, 57–63, 65, 67–69, 71–76, 79–82, 91–93, 95, 113–14, 118, 120, 124
  definition of, 57–60
  feminist, 7, 11–12, 18, 24–27, 31–34, 37, 41, 67–68, 73–74, 82, 91–93, 95, 113–14, 120
  liberation, 24–25, 40, 57, 124
  patriarchal, 11, 15

systematic, 14

Thomas Aquinas, 13, 29, 119

Tradition, 7, 11–13, 19, 22, 26, 29–30, 33–35, 37–39, 45, 47–48, 61–63, 71–72, 74–78, 80–84, 86–87, 90–91, 101, 104, 111, 113, 117

See also Biblical liberating tradition; Christian tradition; Prophetic-liberating tradition; Usable tradition.

Transcendence, 26, 52

Trible, P., 119–20

Trinity, 104, 126

Truth, 63, 79

Truth, S., 105

Universality, 15, 47, 63, 65

Usable language, 42

Usable past, 42, 122

Usable tradition, 32

Vatican Declaration: Women in the Ministerial Priesthood, 96–97, 125

Washbourn, P., 53, 123

Whitehead, A. N., 49–50, 53, 123

Williams, D. S., 121

Wilson-Kastner, P., 122

Witness, Christian, 57–60, 73, 83–85, 87, 92, 101, 104, 107, 111

Women-church, 24, 26–27, 29–31, 36, 39, 68, 112, 121, 127

Women's experience, 7, 12, 14–15, 17, 20–25, 31–32, 35–36, 40, 42–43, 48–69, 72, 76, 79, 81–82, 97, 104, 112, 114, 123

as Christians, 62

bodily, 36, 53–54, 60, 66, 100, 105, 113

definition of, 49–56

feminist, 53, 55–56, 60–61, 66–67, 100, 106

historical, 53, 56, 61, 66–67, 105

individual, 53, 67

norm for theology, 62–67

socialized, 53–55, 60–61, 66, 106

source for theology, 56–62

Word of God, 29, 40, 43–47, 89

Worship, 14, 36, 110, 113